Guidance notes and flow charts for the

Professional Services Short Contract

This contract should be used for the appointment of a consultant to provide professional services. The NEC3 Professional Services Short Contract is an alternative to the NEC3 Professional Services Contract and is for use with contracts which do not require sophisticated management techniques, comprise straightforward work and impose only low risks on both the *Client* and the *Consultant*

An NEC document

April 2013

A partnership between APM and NEC

Construction Clients' Board endorsement of NEC3

The Construction Clients' Board recommends that public sector organisations use the NEC3 contracts when procuring construction. Standardising use of this comprehensive suite of contracts should help to deliver efficiencies across the public sector and promote behaviours in line with the principles of *Achieving Excellence in Construction*.

Cabinet Office UK

NEC is a division of Thomas Telford Ltd, which is a wholly owned subsidiary of the Institution of Civil Engineers (ICE), the owner and developer of the NEC.

The NEC is a family of standard contracts, each of which has these characteristics:

- Its use stimulates good management of the relationship between the two parties to the contract and, hence, of the work included in the contract.

- It can be used in a wide variety of commercial situations, for a wide variety of types of work and in any location.

- It is a clear and simple document – using language and a structure which are straightforward and easily understood.

These guidance notes and flow charts are for the Professional Services Short Contract which is both part of the NEC family and are consistent with all other NEC3 documents.

ISBN (complete box set) 978 0 7277 5867 5
ISBN (this document) 978 0 7277 5919 1
ISBN (Professional Services Short Contract) 978 0 7277 5889 7
ISBN (how to write the PSC Scope) 978 0 7277 5915 3
ISBN (how to use the PSC communication forms) 978 0 7277 5917 7

British Library Cataloguing in Publication Data for this publication is available from the British Library.

Typeset by Academic + Technical, Bristol

Printed and bound in Great Britain by Bell & Bain Limited, Glasgow, UK

CONTENTS

FOREWORD

I was delighted to be asked to write the Foreword for the NEC3 Contracts.

I have followed the outstanding rise and success of NEC contracts for a number of years now, in particular during my tenure as the 146th President of the Institution of Civil Engineers, 2010/11.

In my position as UK Government's Chief Construction Adviser, I am working with Government and industry to ensure Britain's construction sector is equipped with the knowledge, skills and best practice it needs in its transition to a low carbon economy. I am promoting innovation in the sector, including in particular the use of Building Information Modelling (BIM) in public sector construction procurement; and the synergy and fit with the collaborative nature of NEC contracts is obvious. The Government's construction strategy is a very significant investment and NEC contracts will play an important role in setting high standards of contract preparation, management and the desirable behaviour of our industry.

In the UK, we are faced with having to deliver a 15–20 per cent reduction in the cost to the public sector of construction during the lifetime of this Parliament. Shifting mind-set, attitude and behaviour into best practice NEC processes will go a considerable way to achieving this.

Of course, NEC contracts are used successfully around the world in both public and private sector projects; this trend seems set to continue at an increasing pace. NEC contracts are, according to my good friend and NEC's creator Dr Martin Barnes CBE, about better management of projects. This is quite achievable and I encourage you to understand NEC contracts to the best you can and exploit the potential this offers us all.

Peter Hansford

UK Government's Chief Construction Adviser
Cabinet Office

PREFACE

The NEC contracts are the only suite of standard contracts designed to facilitate and encourage good management of the projects on which they are used. The experience of using NEC contracts around the world is that they really make a difference. Previously, standard contracts were written mainly as legal documents best left in the desk drawer until costly and delaying problems had occurred and there were lengthy arguments about who was to blame.

The language of NEC contracts is clear and simple, and the procedures set out are all designed to stimulate good management. Foresighted collaboration between all the contributors to the project is the aim. The contracts set out how the interfaces between all the organisations involved will be managed – from the client through the designers and main contractors to all the many subcontractors and suppliers.

Versions of the NEC contract are specific to the work of professional service providers such as project managers and designers, to main contractors, to subcontractors and to suppliers. The wide range of situations covered by the contracts means that they do not need to be altered to suit any particular situation.

The NEC contracts are the first to deal specifically and effectively with management of the inevitable risks and uncertainties which are encountered to some extent on all projects. Management of the expected is easy, effective management of the unexpected draws fully on the collaborative approach inherent in the NEC contracts.

Most people working on projects using the NEC contracts for the first time are hugely impressed by the difference between the confrontational characteristics of traditional contracts and the teamwork engendered by the NEC. The NEC does not include specific provisions for dispute avoidance. They are not necessary. Collaborative management itself is designed to avoid disputes and it really works.

It is common for the final account for the work on a project to be settled at the time when the work is finished. The traditional long period of expensive professional work after completion to settle final payments just is not needed.

The NEC contracts are truly a massive change for the better for the industries in which they are used.

Dr Martin Barnes CBE

Originator of the NEC contracts

ACKNOWLEDGEMENTS

The first edition of the NEC3 Professional Services Short Contract was produced by the Institution of Civil Engineers. It was drafted in partnership with the Association for Project Management.

The NEC3 Professional Services Short Contract Guidance Notes were produced by the Institution of Civil Engineers and were mainly drafted by R. A. Gerrard with the assistance of P. Higgins. The Flow Charts were produced by Ross Hayes.

The original NEC was designed and drafted by Dr Martin Barnes then of Coopers and Lybrand with the assistance of Professor J. G. Perry then of the University of Birmingham. T W Weddell then of Travers Morgan Management, T H Nicholson, Consultant to the Institution of Civil Engineers, A Norman then of the University of Manchester Institute of Science and Technology and P A Baird, then Corporate Contracts Consultant, Eskom, South Africa.

The drafting members of the project team are:

P Higgins, BSc, CEng, FICE
Jon Broome, BEng, PhD, MAPM, MIoD
Steve Emerton, BSc, MSc, MAPM
Alastair Greenan, BSc, CEng, FIMechE, FIRM, FAPM
Jason Prosser, LLB(Hons) MCIArb

The Institution of Civil Engineers also acknowledges the contribution and feedback from the members of the NEC New Contracts Board, including:

Peer review and assistance from P Higgins, BSc, CEng, FICE with contribution from:

Martin Barnes, BSc(Eng), PhD, FREng, FICE, FCIOB, CCMI, ACIArb, CCMI, ACIArb, MBCS, FInstCES, FAPM
Nigel Shaw, FCIPS, CEng, MIMechE
Mark Lomas, APM Hong Kong
Lindsay Scott, APM
Stuart Dixon, APM

INTRODUCTION

| The notes in boxes like this one | printed within the NEC Professional Services Short Contract (PSSC), explain how to complete PSSC when it is used for a simple, low risk contract. These boxed notes are reproduced in these guidance notes, which also explain the background to the PSSC and give guidance for its use as a main contract. The flow charts show the procedural logic on which the PSSC is based and are published in this volume for reference.

In these guidance notes, as in the contract itself, terms which are defined in the PSSC have capital initials and those which are identified in the Contract Data are in italics. The guidance notes and the flow charts are not part of the PSSC and have no legal function.

WHEN TO USE THE PSSC

Within the NEC family, the PSSC is the alternative to the Professional Services Contract (PSC) and is for use with contracts which

- do not require sophisticated management techniques,
- comprise straightforward work and
- impose only low risks on both the *Client* and the *Consultant*.

This has been expressed as 'a simpler approach to simpler commissions'. Users choosing between the PSSC and the PSC should base their choice purely on the level of complexity of the work required and the level of risk to each of the Parties. As such the PSSC can be used for any low risk professional services commission, in whatever sector and in whatever country. This includes:

- Non-UK based commissions and those outside the NEC3 contract families 'home' sector of heavy engineering and construction where it is widely and successfully used.
- Appointing a consultant as a character in another member of the NEC3 family. For example, the *Project Manager* or *Supervisor* in the NEC3 Engineering and Construction Contract or *Service Manager* in the NEC3 Term Service Contract. Where this is the case, the Scope will be to carry out the actions in the relevant contract, with any further constraints and reporting requirements also stated.
- Appointing a consultant to contribute to any project or contract (whether an NEC3 contract or not). This includes an appointment of a project manager and the PSSC replaces the Association for Project Management's Standard Terms published in 1998.

- Professional advice delivered on an 'as and when needed' basis, where services are instructed through the compensation event procedure.
- A range of payment mechanisms which are:
  - defined services paid for as a series of completed activities;
  - services which are defined in terms of what the *Consultant* has to do, but not in terms of the quantity of work which has to be done. In which case, the *Consultant* is paid for the quantity of work done multiplied by their tendered rates; or
  - payment on a time charge basis where the *Consultant* is paid on the basis of tendered rate per unit of time multiplied by the time that they either take or, in the case of called off work, are forecast to take to do the work.

NEC3 contracts

The current list of published NEC3 contracts is stated below:

- NEC3 Engineering and Construction Contract (ECC)
- NEC3 Engineering and Construction Subcontract (ECS)
- NEC3 Engineering and Construction Short Contract (ECSC)
- NEC3 Engineering and Construction Short Subcontract (ECSS)
- NEC3 Professional Services Contract (PSC)
- NEC3 Professional Services Short Contract (PSSC)
- NEC3 Term Service Contract (TSC)
- NEC3 Term Service Short Contract (TSSC)
- NEC3 Supply Contract (SC)
- NEC3 Supply Short Contract (SSC)
- NEC3 Framework Contract (FC)
- NEC3 Adjudicator's Contract (AC)

For general guidance on when to use each contract refer to the NEC3 Procurement and Contract Strategies guide, available on www.neccontract.com.

THE PSSC PACKAGE

The PSSC package includes the conditions of contract and forms which, when filled in, make up a complete contract. The forms are on pages 1 to 9 of the package and are provided for

- the title page and the Contract Forms comprising
- Contract Data
- The *Consultant*'s Offer,
- The *Client*'s Acceptance,
- Price List and
- Scope.

Stage A: How a *Client* invites tenders for a job

Examples using a fictitious training commission are appended to these notes to illustrate how the title page and Contract Forms should be filled in at each of the following three stages leading to a contract.

The *Client* uses the package to invite tenders for proposed *services* by providing the following information on the forms and sending the package to tenderers with the invitation to tender.

- **The title page (page 1) – see example A1**
- **Contract Data (pages 2–4) – see example A2**
- **The *Consultant*'s Offer and the *Client*'s Acceptance (pages 5 & 6) – leave blank**
- **Price List (page 7) – see notes on clause 50.2**

In the Price List, entries in the first four columns are made either by the *Client* or the tenderer.

For each row:

- If the *Consultant* is to be paid an amount for the item which is not adjusted if the quantity of work in the item changes, then the tenderer enters the amount in the Price column only.
- If the *Consultant* is to be paid an amount for the item of work and which is the rate for the work multiplied by the quantity completed, the tenderer enters the rate which is then multiplied by the Expected quantity to produce the Price, which is also entered.
- If the work is to be paid on a time charge basis, only expenses should be included and enter 'Not Applicable' in 'The offered total of the Prices' in 'The *Consultant*'s Offer'.

Costs incurred by the *Consultant* other than the listed expenses are included in the Rates and Prices and the *staff rates*. If expenses are paid at cost, then 'at cost' should be entered into the Rate column.

Any unused rows in the Price List template should be deleted or struck through.

- **Scope (pages 8–10) (see notes on clauses 11.2(8) and 60.1(1))**

> The Scope should be a complete and precise statement of the *Client*'s requirements. If it is incomplete or imprecise, there is a risk that the *Consultant* will interpret it differently from the *Client*'s intention. Information provided by the *Consultant* should be listed in the Scope only if the *Client* is satisfied that it is required, is part of a complete statement of the *Client*'s requirements and is consistent with other parts of the Scope.

1 Purpose of the *services*

> Provide a brief summary of why the *services* are being commissioned and what they will be used for.

2 Description of the *services*

> Give a complete and precise description of what the *Consultant* is required to do.
>
> If items of work have to be provided by a stated date, include a table describing the work and stating the date when it is to be provided.

3 Existing information

> List existing information which is relevant to the *services*. This can include documents which the *Consultant* is to further develop.

4 Specifications and standards

> List any specifications and standards that apply to this contract.

It is important that these are thoroughly prepared and comprehensive because the PSSC definition of a Defect (clause 11.2(4)) is based entirely on the Scope or the applicable law. Include in the specifications details of

- quality standards for deliverables,
- any checking procedures required and
- any other specific requirements.

5 Constraints on how the *Consultant* is to Provides the Services

> State any constraints on sequence and timing of work and on the method and conduct of work including the requirements for any work by the *Client*.
>
> Set out any requirements for a quality management system.
>
> Include a dispute resolution procedure if required.

Refer to any specific constraints relating to the country where the *services* are to be provided. These may include provisions such as a labour intensive approach using appropriate technology, and maximising local employment.

The *Consultant* should be allowed to subcontract work without any limit (clause 22.1). However, the *Client* may wish to limit the extent of subcontracting if, for example, the *Consultant* is being selected for a particular expertise. The *Client* may also wish to provide lists of subconsultants who would be acceptable for specific categories of work. Any such constraints should be stated here.

If the *Consultant*'s work needs to be co-ordinated with other activities or contracts, define the parts of the *services* affected and state the dates by which each is to be completed.

If the *Consultant*'s work is to be affected by work done by the *Client*, the nature of the *Client*'s work, including the timing should be stated.

If the *Consultant* is to work to a quality management system, then this should be described here.

If a dispute resolution procedure is required, this should be stated here.

6 Requirements for the programme

> State whether a programme is required and, if it is, state what form it is to be in, what information is to be shown on it, when it is to be submitted and when it is to be updated.

The programme is an important document for administering the contract. It informs the *Client* of the *Consultant*'s detailed intentions of how and at what times he is to Provide the Services. It enables the *Client* to monitor the *Consultant*'s performance and to assess the effects of compensation events.

7 Information and other things provided by the *Client*

> Describe what information and other things the *Client* is to provide and by when. Information is that which is not currently available, but will become available during the contract. Other things could include access to a person, place (such as office space or a site) or the *Client*'s information technology systems.

Each item should be stated together with the date by which it will be provided.

Invitation to tender

In the *Client*'s invitation to tender, there may be included a number of matters, for example

- any constraints on how the Price List should be used for the submission of tenders,
- if the *Client* requires tenderers to give details of methods to be used in Providing the Service, the information should be requested in the invitation to tender,
- in some circumstances the *Client* may also wish to draw the attention of tenderers to local employment legislation and health and safety legislation and may also emphasise the importance of gender equality (equal opportunities, equal pay for work of equal value), minimum age of employment and protection of wages (to ensure wages are paid on time and in cash).

Stage B: How a tenderer makes an offer

A tenderer uses the package to make an offer by providing information on the following forms.

- Price List (page 7) – see notes under Stage A and on clause 50.3.
- The *Consultant*'s Offer (pages 5 & 6) – see example B1.

Enter the total of the Prices from the Price List (unless payment is to be made on a time charge basis).

The tenderer's covering letter should also include

- any extra Scope proposed by the tenderer and
- any additional information asked for by the *Client* in the invitation to tender, such details of methods to be used.

The letter should also make it clear if any part of the *Consultant*'s Offer does not comply with the Contract Data or the Scope provided by the *Client*.

Stage C: How a contract is made

The package becomes the complete contract document when the *Client* makes the following additional entries and sends a copy to the *Consultant* who has made the chosen offer.

- The *Client*'s Acceptance of the offer (page 6) – see example C1.
- The title page (page 1) – *Consultant*'s name added – see example C2.
- The Contract Forms including the Contract Data (page 3) – see example C3.

Under the law of England and Wales, the contract between the *Client* and the *Consultant* is then made. There may be other requirements in other jurisdictions.

The PSSC uses a simple offer (The *Consultant*'s Offer, pages 4 & 5) and acceptance (The *Client*'s Acceptance, page 5) to create a contract. It is emphasised that this is the most efficient and clear way of creating a simple contract and users should aim to achieve this. However, if

- the tenderer's covering letter requires changes to the documents or
- the *Client* has issued supplements to the invitation to tender amending the documents,

these need to be recorded with the *Consultant*'s Offer or the *Client*'s Acceptance.

The *Client* adding into the *Client*'s Acceptance before this is achieved either by

- the tenderer adding after the offered total of the Prices

'This offer includes our covering letter

Reference . . . . Dated . . . . 'or

- the signature

'The Offer includes the information provided in . . . . '.

(This is either the tenderer's covering letter if not already mentioned in the *Consultant*'s Offer or a document or summary agreed by the two parties after the tender was received.)

NOTES ON THE CLAUSES

1 General

Actions 10

10.1 This clause obliges the *Client* and the *Consultant* to do everything which the contract states each of them does. It is the only clause which uses the future tense. For simplicity, everything else is in the present tense.

Identified and defined 11
terms

11.1 The Contract Data is used to complete the contract by identifying terms in italics and providing the information that certain clauses state is in the Contract Data (see examples A2, B1 and C3).

11.2 The meanings of all defined terms are given in this clause.

11.2(1) In order to have a clear definition of Completion for a particular job, the *Client*'s intended use of the completed works needs to be clear. This is one of the reasons why the *Client* needs to state in the Scope what that intention is. (See notes on Scope part 5 under 'Stage A: How a *Client* invites tenders for a job'.)

11.2(2) The Completion Date is the date by which the *Consultant* is required to achieve Completion (clauses 11.2(1) and 30.1). At the start of a contract it is stated in the Contract Data as the *completion date* but it may be changed as a result of a compensation event (clauses 62.1 and 63.3).

11.2(3) Any departure from the *services* as specified in the contract, or from the applicable law, constitutes a Defect.

11.2(5) Prices may comprise lump sums, quantity related items and/or on a time charge basis.

11.2(6) One use of this definition of 'Provide the Services' in conjunction with the 'Scope' (11.2(8)) is to establish the *Consultant*'s main obligation in clause 21.1.

11.2(7) The Scope is the *Client*'s statement of what the *Consultant* is required to do in Providing the Services and what constraints the *Consultant* must comply with (clause 21.1). The Scope document provided with the invitation to tender will be the basis of the *Consultant*'s tender and must be as comprehensive as possible (see notes on Scope under 'Stage A: How a *Client* invites tenders for a job').

The definition includes not only material contained in the document called 'Scope' but also instructions issued under the terms of the contract. The *Client* may instruct a change to the Scope document issued under clause 20.2; this will then be a compensation event (clause 60.1(1)).

The PSSC can be used to call off work when required by issuing instructions which add the work into the Scope. Initially, the Scope would identify the work to be carried out when instructed, and describe the procedure to be followed when such work is required. The instruction to add the work is a compensation event, and including items for potential work in the Price List would allow the assessment of the instructed work to use the rates fixed at the Contract Date.

The Law	**12**	
	12.3	Orally agreed changes to the contract have no effect unless they are followed up by the procedures stated in this clause.
Communications	**13**	
	13.2	This clause allows both the *Client* and *Consultant* to delegate many of their actions to other people who will act on their behalf. It is also good contractual practice for both Parties to be absolutely clear who they can and cannot give contractual instructions to, or receive them from.
	13.3	The *period for reply*, stated in the Contract Data (example A2), aims to achieve a timely turn round of communications. Its length depends on the particular circumstances of the contract but would normally be one or two weeks. Other periods for specific actions are stated in the relevant clauses e.g. clause 61.1 – submission of quotations for compensation events. All such periods can be changed only by agreement between the Parties.
	13.4	This clause makes clear that acceptance by the *Client* of the *Consultant*'s communication or his work does not result in a transfer of liability.
Early warning	**14**	
	14.1	The obligation which this clause requires of both Parties is intended to bring into the open as early as possible any matter which could adversely affect the successful outcome of the contract. Both Parties should give early warning in order to maximise the time available for taking avoiding action.
	14.2	The Parties are required to co-operate in giving priority to solving the problem, irrespective of how the problem has been caused and who carries financial responsibility for it. Any discussion between the Parties should concentrate on solving the problem. The purpose of the Parties' discussions is not to decide responsibility or who will pay for the actions taken as the relevant provisions of the contract will cover these aspects quite adequately.

2 The *Parties*' main responsibilities

The *Client*'s obligations **20**

20.1 This clause relates to the information and other things stated in the Scope. The *Client*'s failure to take an action within the time required may result in a compensation event arising (clause 60.1(2)).

20.2 Only the *Client*, or an authorised delegate of the *Client* (clause 13.2), can change the Scope.

20.3 This clause recognises the professional nature of the *services* being provided. If the *Client*'s instructions cannot be complied with, the *Consultant* should advise the *Client* of the fact and suggest alternative measures to achieve the *Client*'s requirements.

The *Consultant*'s obligations **21**

21.1 This clause states the *Consultant*'s basic obligation. 'Provide the Services' is defined in clause 11.2(7). It includes supplying all necessary resources to achieve the end result. It demonstrates the importance of thoroughly prepared and comprehensive Scope (see notes on Scope under 'Stage A: How a *Client* invites tenders for a job').

21.2 This clause states the level of skill and care required of the *Consultant*. It follows that a Defect may not necessarily be the liability of the *Consultant*.

21.3 Various clauses in the contract give the *Client* authority to issue instructions to the *Consultant*. These instructions should be given within the limits and for the reasons expressly stated. If for any reason the *Consultant* disagrees with an instruction, having exhausted the procedures in the contract for dealing with such a situation, his remedy is to follow the dispute resolution procedure in clause 93 as appropriate. He should not refuse to obey the instruction.

Subcontracting and people **22**

22.1 As in other NEC contracts, the PSSC does not provide for nominated subcontractors. The *Consultant* has full responsibility for Providing the Services, whether subcontracted or not (see notes on Scope under 'Stage A: How a *Client* invites tenders for a job').

22.2 The key people named in the Contract Data should be the persons named by the *Consultant* to do the jobs most critical to Providing the Services. The *Consultant* can only replace a key person if the qualifications and experience of a replacement person are as good of the person who being replaced, and this is accepted by the *Client*.

22.3 The *Client* has authority to have a *Consultant*'s employee removed from work on the contract. Possible reasons for exercising this authority may include

- poor work
- security
- health and safety
- disorderly behaviour affecting the *Client*'s activities.

3 Time

Starting and Completion | **30**

30.1 The *starting date* is stated in the Contract Data. If the procurement process and appointment of the *Consultant* takes longer than anticipated, it may be necessary to adjust the *starting date* by agreement before signing the *Client*'s Acceptance. The Completion Date may be changed from the *completion date* as a result of a compensation event. It is essential that a *completion date* is stated in the Contract Data. If this is not done, the time effects of compensation events cannot be applied.

30.2 The *Client* is responsible for certifying Completion, as defined in clause 11.2(1), within one week of it being achieved.

30.3 This clause gives the *Client* authority to control the stopping and re-starting of work for any reason, for example, where there is a risk of injury to people or damage to property, or the works may no longer be required. An instruction given under this clause constitutes a compensation event (clause 60.1(3)). But if it arises from a fault of the *Consultant*, the Prices are not changed.

The programme | **31**

31.1 The *Client*'s requirements for the *Consultant*'s programme should be stated in the Scope (see notes on Scope under 'Stage A: How a *Client* invites tenders for a job'). Some *Client*s may require tenderers to submit a programme with their tenders. The *Consultant*'s programme is an important document for administering the contract. It informs the *Client* of the *Consultant*'s detailed intentions of how he is to Provide the Services. It enables the *Client* to monitor the *Consultant*'s performance and to assess the effects of compensation events. The *Client* should think carefully about what is required for them to do this, yet at the same time not overload the *Consultant* with other obligations.

4 Quality

Quality management system **40**

40.1 This clause provides for the *Consultant* to operate a quality management to system to the extent required by the Scope.

The *Client* decides the extent of the quality management system. On one extreme he may require no formal quality management system. On the other extreme he may require the operation of a fully certified quality assurance system under ISO standards. The quality management system required of the *Consultant* should recognise the equivalent requirements on other consultants or contractors and be compatible with them.

Notifying Defects **41**

41.1 The definition of a Defect (clause 11.2(4)) is based entirely on the Scope. If the *Client* is not satisfied with work for a reason other than that it is not in accordance with the Scope, then it is not a Defect. In order to 'correct' the work, the *Client* would need to instruct a change to the Scope, and this would be a compensation event (clause 60.1(1)).

The period between Completion and the *defects date* is stated in the Contract Data. The length of the period will depend on the type of *services* being provided, but will normally be between six months and a year. This clause requires each Party to notify the other of each Defect found until the *defects date*.

41.2 The *Consultant* is required to notify uncorrected Defects at Completion (clause 11.2(1)).

41.3 This clause preserves the *Client*'s rights under law in relation to Defects which are not discovered until after the *defects date*.

Correcting Defects **42**

42.1 This clause requires the *Consultant* to correct all Defects, i.e. so that the *services* are in accordance with the Scope (clause 11.2(8)).

42.2 There is no fixed time within which the *Consultant* is required to correct a Defect or make good an omission. This will depend on the circumstances of each particular case. The test to be applied in each case is 'Within what time will the Defect or omission and its correction or making good, cause the minimum adverse effect on the *Client* or others who are using the *services*?'. It does not require any admission by the *Consultant* of responsibility for the Defect but enables the *services* to be corrected with appropriate urgency to minimise disruption to the *Client*'s project.

This clause also states the action that the *Client* may take if the *Consultant* fails to correct a Defect in accordance with the contract.

5 Payment

Assessing the amount due 50

50.1 The *Client*'s statement in the Contract Data fixes an *assessment day* in each month from the *starting date* until the month after the *defects date*. This provides for a monthly assessment by the *Consultant* even when the amount due may be nil.

The *Consultant* assesses the amount due by each *assessment day* and uses the assessment to apply to the *Client* for payment.

50.2 The *Consultant* is required to submit an invoice for the change in the amount due since the previous invoice and provide the details to show how the amount due has been assessed. The 'amount due' is the total payment due to date. The *Consultant*'s invoice is for the change in the amount due since the last payment.

50.3 The payment mechanism is largely based on the use of the Price List and the Prices.

The Price List included in the contract provides the pricing information needed for assessing the amount due. Notes on how to use the Price List are included under its heading in the PSSC and are repeated in these notes under 'Stage A: How a *Client* invites tenders for a job'.

The Prices are defined in clause 11.2(6). The second sentence of the definition provides for the pricing of those items for which a quantity and a rate are stated in the Price List.

Payments for an item in the Price List do not become due until the work described in the item has been completed unless a quantity and a rate are stated, in which case only the Price for the quantity of work completed is included.

For work carried out on a time charge basis, payments are based on the time expended on work which has been completed multiplied by the appropriate *staff rate*. The *staff rates* are stated in the *Consultant*'s Offer and the *Consultant* is paid in addition those expenses stated in the Price List.

The Price List provides for flexibility in tendering methods including items which

a) the *Client* describes and for which the tenderer quotes a Price,
b) the *Client* describes with a quantity and for which the tenderer quotes a rate extended to a Price (adjustable to quantity completed),
c) the *Client* describes and the tenderer breaks down into sub-items comprising a mixture of a) and b), each of which the tenderer quotes for,
d) the *Client* describes and the tenderer quotes for a list of the activities necessary to complete the item, each with a Price,
e) the tenderer describes and quotes Prices or rates in accordance with the notes at the head of the Price List and the invitation to tender, or
f) the *Client* wishes to pay for work on a time charge basis.

The *Client* should include in the invitation to tender any constraints on how the Price List should be used for the submission of tenders.

It is important that item descriptions are carefully written with appropriate references to the Scope. For quantity related items, the work to be covered by the rate must be clearly stated. If there is a risk of differing interpretations on how an item is measured, the basis of measurement should be included in the item description of the Price List.

The fourth bullet in clause 50.3 refers to other amounts to be added or deducted in order to calculate the amount due. Amounts added may include interest on late payments and deductions may include such things as *delay damages*.

It is recommended that the Parties should agree, at the start of the contract, how the administration of sales tax documentation should be dealt with as part of the payment procedure.

No provision is made for inflation. In some countries where inflation is high the *Client* may wish to take the risk of price increases beyond a pre-determined threshold. This could be provided for in the additional conditions.

No provision has been made for advanced payments. If the *Client* is prepared to make an advanced payment, a separate item should be included in the Price List. The item must describe how the advanced payment is repaid.

The amount due also includes the listed expenses incurred by the *Consultant* in Providing the Services. The items of expenses that can be recovered by the *Consultant* are listed in the Price List. Any expenses not so defined are not directly reimbursed to the *Consultant*, who must therefore make due allowance for them in pricing his offer, i.e. in the Rates and Prices and the *staff rates*. Consequently, if the *Client* wishes to reimburse only a few certain costs directly, then he should state these in the Price List and delete or strike through any remaining rows. If he only wishes to reimburse them at cost, then he should state 'at cost' in the 'rate' column. For items such as car mileage, a rate per mile or kilometre would normally be stated. It is for the *Client* and not the tenderer to decide in the Price List which expenses are recoverable. All tenderers will then bid on the same basis, making assessment more straightforward.

Items of expenses which may be included in the Price List are photocopies, telephone, facsimile and package costs, postage, travel and hotel costs. Details of travel costs by public transport or private car should also be included as required.

Expenses should also include disbursements, which are fees and charges paid by the *Consultant* on behalf of the *Client*. Any such items which the *Client* requires the *Consultant* to arrange for and pay, e.g. fees for planning applications or advertising for site staff, should be listed as expenses in the Price List and stated as corresponding obligations of the *Consultant* in the Scope.

Pricing of expenses may be expressed in various forms. These include

- at cost
- at cost plus . . . . percent
- lump sums and rates
- percentage of the Prices.

50.4 Where the *Client* is not in agreement with an invoice submitted by the *Consultant*, he has to

- notify the *Consultant* of the correction and
- explain to the *Consultant* his reasons for each correction.

The *Consultant* then has to correct the invoice to a sum agreed by the *Client* or provide further information to justify the invoice already submitted. While the disagreement is being resolved the *Client* should pay what he considers the proper amount in respect of the *services* provided. This will include substituting his assessment for the *Consultant*'s invoice in respect of that part of the *services* he disagrees with. If he fails to make payment he will be liable to pay interest to the *Consultant* on any delayed payment (clause 51.2).

50.5 The *delay damages* to be stated in the Contract Data (see example A2) are the amount to be paid by the *Consultant* to the *Client* if the *Consultant* fails to complete the works by the Completion Date. The *delay damages* should be set at a level which the applicable law will enforce. For example, under the law of England and Wales, the amount of *delay damages* must not exceed a genuine pre-estimate of the damage that would be suffered by the *Client* as a result of the delay to Completion. In that case, the *Client* should keep a record of the calculation of the pre-estimate. When preparing the tender document, if the *Client* does not wish to deduct delay damages from the *Consultant* in the event of delay by the *Consultant*, then 'Nil' should be stated in the Contract Data.

Having calculated the maximum level of damages, the *Client* may wish to put damages for a lesser amount in the contract as excessive damages from the *Consultant*'s point of view may cause them to

- raise their Prices to cover the risk of having to pay *delay damages* and
- if late, resort to defensive behaviour putting blame on the *Client* for any delay in order to avoid having to pay the damages, instead of focussing on resolving the issues causing the delay.

Payment 51

51.1 The latest date for payment is related to the *assessment day* which occurs after the *Client* receives the *Consultant*'s invoice.

51.2 For simplicity, a fixed rate of interest of 0.5% per week is stated for the calculation of interest due on late payments, with an option for the *Client* to state a different rate in the Contract Data.

6 Compensation events

Compensation events	**60**	As in other NEC contracts, compensation events are those events stated in the contract to be compensation events. If an event is not so stated, it is not a compensation event and is at the *Consultant*'s financial risk. If a compensation event occurs and does not arise from the *Consultant*'s fault, the *Consultant* may be compensated for any effect the event has on cost and the Completion Date.
	60.1	Events which are compensation events in the PSSC are listed in this clause. Any additional compensation events required for a particular contract should be stated in an additional condition of contract in the Contract Data.
	60.1(1)	This clause embodies the principle that a tender can only be based on the information the tenderer has when the tender is prepared. Scope as defined in clause 11.2(8) comprises the document called 'Scope' together with any instructions issued under the contract.
	60.1(2)	This relates to the *Client*'s obligation in various clauses to take an action within the time required by the contract. This could include failure by the *Client* in clause 20.1 to provide information and other things which the contract requires him to provide by the dates stated in the Scope or a later date if agreed. It also includes the failure of the *Client* to reply within one week of the *Consultant*'s submission of a notified compensation event (clause 62.3) or providing a certificate within the *period for reply* from the insurer or broker stating that the insurances required by the contract are in force (clause 81.2).
	60.1(3)	This clause relates to the *Client*'s authority in clause 30.3 to stop or not to start any work.
	60.1(4)	The *Client* is able to change a decision made under the contract.
		Any compensation events other than those identified in clause 60.1 that are required for a specific contract should be stated in an additional condition of contract in the Contract Data. For example, if there is a significant risk of an increase in the cost of people due to changes in the law, the occurrence of such a change could be made a compensation event. Any risk which it is prudent for the *Client* to carry can be dealt with in this way.
Notifying compensation events	**61**	
	61.1	Both the *Client* or and the *Consultant* are obliged to notify compensation events to the other.
	61.2	This clause states the period within which the *Consultant* is required to submit his quotation, when a compensation event is notified by the *Client*. The *Client* would normally instruct the *Consultant* to submit a quotation at the same time as notifying the *Consultant* of a compensation event. Where the *Consultant* notifies a compensation event, then he submits a quotation at the same time. The timely aspects in this clause are is intended to expedite the procedure, so that dealing with compensation events a long time after they have occurred is avoided.
	61.3	This clause puts time limits on when the *Consultant* can notify a compensation event, again to expedite the procedure.

Quotations for compensation events	**62**	
	62.1	This clause describes what a quotation for a compensation event is to comprise. The *Consultant* should include in his quotation proposed changes to the Prices or rates and Completion Date. The *Consultant* must also submit details of his assessment with each quotation, including any assumptions. The assumptions are provided so that the *Client* can decide the best way to deal with them – acceptance, delay the assessment or make his own assessment.

62.2 This clause states the actions to be taken by the *Client* within one week of a compensation event being notified by the *Consultant*. If the *Client* decides that a notified event is not a compensation event, or arises from the fault of the *Consultant*, the compensation event procedure does not continue. If the Parties cannot resolve their differences, then the *Consultant* may ultimately decide to use the dispute resolution procedure.

If the *Client* decides that a notified event is a compensation event, he replies in one of three ways. The *Client* could

- notify his acceptance of the quotation,
- notify that he does not agree with the quotation and then notifies the *Consultant* of his own assessment or
- state that the effect of a compensation event is too uncertain to be forecast reasonably and notifies the *Consultant* of the date when the compensation event assessment is to be made.

An example of when the *Client* may decide to delay the assessment would be where a planning consent has been delayed; the assessment is made when progress to the next stage can be made. A firm date should always be identified; this can be further deferred if necessary, but it avoids the risk of the event being overlooked.

62.3 If the *Consultant* fails to provide a quotation, as is required by clause 61.2, the *Client* notifies his own assessment of the compensation event. If the *Consultant* disagrees with this assessment and the Parties cannot resolve their differences, then the *Consultant* may ultimately decide to use the dispute resolution procedure.

62.4 If the *Client* notifies the *Consultant* of the assessment of a compensation event, then he should also include details of his assessment at that time.

Assessing compensation events	**63**	Clause 63 states how the effects of compensation events on the Prices are assessed. This is the same whether the assessment is done by the *Consultant*, the *Client* or under the dispute resolution procedure.

63.1 This clause describes the assessment procedure used when the compensation event affects only the quantities of work to be done under items in the Price List for which a quantity and rate are stated. For simplicity, the rates in the Price List are used to price the changed quantities.

63.2 This clause states the procedure used for all other compensation events. The changes to the Prices are assessed by forecasting the effect of the compensation event on the cost of Providing the Services. This is unless the compensation event has already occurred, in which case the assessment is based upon the cost due to the event which the *Consultant* has incurred. In the compensation event assessment, the *staff rates* are used together with any appropriate expenses from the Price List. The cost of preparing quotations for a compensation event is specifically excluded from the assessment of that compensation event. The *Consultant* should therefore allow for these costs in tendered *staff rates*.

63.3   If the *Consultant*'s planned Completion is delayed by the forecast effect of a compensation event, the Completion Date is delayed by the same period. If the effect of a compensation event is to affect a date stated in the Scope by which an item of work has to be provided, then the *Client* must also instruct a change to that date.

63.4   This clause is intended to encourage the *Consultant* to notify early warnings. Not giving an early warning under clause 14.1 could reduce the amount of time and, in many situations, options available to minimise or avoid additional cost or time. As any resulting compensation event is assessed 'as if' the *Consultant* had given an early warning, it would reduce the assessment. Hence, any additional costs and time incurred through the *Consultant* not giving an early warning when they could have done would fall to the *Consultant*.

63.5   This clause is intended to protect the *Client* against inefficiency on the part of the *Consultant*.

63.6   The value of compensation events are added to the Price List.

63.7   This clause emphasises the finality of the assessment of compensation events. If the forecast of the effect on cost included in the accepted or notified assessment proves to be wrong when the work is done, the assessment is not changed.

7 Rights to material

The Parties' use of material | **70**

70.1   Under this clause, the *Consultant* retains rights over material provided by him, but the *Client* may use it for the purposes stated in the Scope. The clause is drafted in general terms and may not involve such rights as designers' copyright. The *Consultant* may reasonably insist that any re-use of material which he provides is entirely at the *Client*'s risk, unless the *Client* obtains prior verification by the *Consultant*. The *Consultant* may further seek indemnity from the *Client* against claims arising from such re-use. This emphasises the importance of the drafting of the Scope, to make clear liabilities for use or re-use by the *Client* of material produced by the *Consultant*.

70.2   This clause prohibits the *Consultant* from using any material provided by the *Client* for his own purposes or for purposes other than for Providing the Services.

70.3   Confidentiality is achieved by the provisions of this clause. The *Consultant* may, however, publicise certain information, provided he obtains the *Client*'s agreement under clause 71.1.

70.4   The *Consultant* may use material produced under this contract for other work. Exceptions are stated in the Scope.

8 Indemnity, insurance and liability

The method of dealing with the *Client*'s and *Consultant*'s risks used in the PSSC is different to the approach in the PSC.

The *Consultant*'s liability to Provide the Services is stated in the PSSC in clause 21.1. Certain financial risks, however, constitute compensation events in clause 60.1. Additional conditions stated in the Contract Data may include further compensation events.

Limitation of liability **80**

80.1 This clause protects the *Client* in the event that the *Consultant* infringes the rights of others who may seek redress from the *Client*. The only exception is when the *Client* himself provides things for the *Consultant*'s use.

Insurance cover **81**

81.1 Both the *Client*'s and the *Consultant*'s responsibility for providing insurances is stated in this clause. The insurances they each provide and the periods of cover are stated in the Contract Data.

Three main types of insurance are required.

(a) Professional indemnity insurance
This is the first insurance stated in the Contract Data, and provides for insurance cover in respect of any sum which the *Consultant* may become legally liable to pay arising out of claims made against him during the period of insurance as a result of any neglect, error or omission in carrying out his professional activities.

The level of cover is to be stated in the Contract Data. In some circumstances, some insurers insist on a maximum sum for any one claim and in the aggregate on the period of insurance.

The period for which insurance cover is required is also to be stated in the Contract Data. Claims in respect of professional indemnity insurance normally have to be made during the period of insurance. Claims cannot normally be made after the period of insurance even though the act of neglect may have taken place during the period of insurance. Thus, in dealing with the period of cover, it is desirable that the policy is kept in force after completion of the *services* to deal with claims made in respect of negligent acts which do not manifest themselves until sometime after. To provide adequate cover in these circumstances, the period stated should be the relevant legal limitation period after Completion.

(b) Public liability insurance
This is the second insurance in the Contract Data and provides insurance cover for the *Consultant* against his legal liability for damages arising from bodily injury to or death of a person (other than the *Consultant*'s employees) or loss of or damage to property occurring during the period of insurance. In this type of insurance, the act of neglect leading to liability has to take place during the currency of the policy, but claims can be made afterwards. Hence there is no need to maintain the policy after Completion.

(c) Employer's liability insurance
The third insurance in the Contract Data provides insurance cover for legal liability for bodily injury to or death of the *Consultant*'s employees arising out of or in the course of their employment. Employers in many countries are required by law to insure employees for personal injury and death. This insurance is compulsory in the United Kingdom, the statutory provisions requiring insurance for a minimum amount for each occurrence. Elsewhere in the world other regulations may apply, requiring workmen's compensation-type coverage or participation in state social security schemes. Insurance cover may terminate on Completion.

The *Client* is required to state in the Contract Data the extent of the insurances the *Client* is providing (if any) and the minimum level of cover for the three insurances in the Contract Data.

81.2   Insurers and brokers will generally not release copies of consultants' insurance policies. It is normal, however, for the *Consultant* to provide a certificate from his broker confirming that he does hold the insurances. In the same way, the *Client* is required to provide a certificate on request confirming that he holds the necessary insurances.

Limitation of liability   **82**

82.1   The *Consultant*'s total liabilities to the *Client* (i.e. the maximum the *Client* could recover a breach of contract) will be the amount stated in the Contract Data. The contract divides these maximum liabilities into two groups, those for which the *Consultant* is required to insure for which there will be a relatively high cap – for instance, a million pounds – and those for which he is not required in the contract to insure (and, in any case, is unlikely to be able to gain insurance) such as for *delay damages*. For the latter, the cap on liability is likely to be significantly lower and should reflect would the *Consultant* is able to afford – otherwise they could become insolvent and the *Client* may well become one of many creditors.

82.2   If the *Consultant* is found to be legally liable along with others, the *Consultant*'s liability to the *Client* is limited to his proportionate failure. If, for example, a court were to conclude that a consultant appointed as a *Consultant* under the PSSC to carry out the design for a construction contract was 15% liable, and the contractor 85% liable for the *Client*'s losses, the maximum the *Client* could recover from the *Consultant* would be 15% of his losses up to the limit of insurance or other figure stated.

9 Termination and dispute resolution

Termination and reasons for termination 90

90.1 Both the *Client* and *Consultant* have rights to terminate the *Consultant*'s obligations under the contract in certain circumstances. This termination does not terminate the contract itself. The *Consultant* does no further work after termination.

90.2 Under this clause, the *Client* may terminate only for the two reasons stated. The first is where the *Client* no longer requires the *services*, for any reason, and the second covers the situation where the *Consultant* has defaulted and not put this right within a stated period.

90.3 The *Consultant* may terminate only for the particular reason stated, which relates to lack of payment by the *Client*.

Procedures on termination 91

91.1 This clause covers the work required following termination to achieve an orderly close-down of the *Consultant*'s *services*. It is possible that in certain circumstances material provided by the *Consultant* is later revised by the *Client* for purposes which are not appropriate but over which the *Consultant* has no control. If such circumstances are likely to occur, liability of the Parties should be made clear in the contract.

91.2 After termination, the *Consultant* must hand over to the *Client* all material he was preparing for him under the contract but the *Consultant* is entitled to keep the material until he has been paid. Any dispute over the amount of the final payment would go through the adjudication process.

The *Client* will secure title to any materials when the *Client* has paid for them. This will be achieved by the payment on termination (see clause 92.1).

Payment on termination 92

92.1 This clause lists the components of cost that are always included in the amount due on termination.

92.2 This clause state further components which are included in the amount due when termination has occurred for a particular reason, being insolvency or default by the *Consultant*.

Dispute resolution 93

93.1 This clause requires the Parties to follow any procedure for dispute resolution if it is stated in the Scope. This may be a form of mediation, conciliation or adjudication. In some countries, the legal system fixes a specific procedure for dispute resolution; in that case the Scope should incorporate that procedure. If there is no procedure in the Scope, either Party may refer a dispute straight to the *tribunal*. The *Client* identifies the *tribunal* in the Contract Data (see example A2). The choice will normally be between arbitration and the courts, either being competent to give a legally final and binding decision on the dispute. It is important to be aware of the different choices that are available when making the decision about the *tribunal*. Different laws and arbitration procedures exist in different countries, whilst in some countries no arbitration exists at all. If the *tribunal* is arbitration, the arbitration procedure to be used is also stated in the Contract Data (see example A2).

It is important for the Parties to understand that dispute resolution processes should only be used after attempts at negotiations have failed. They should not be seen as an alternative to the Parties reaching agreement on their disputes, either through informal negotiation, or via other more formal non-binding processes such as mediation or conciliation.

93.2   This clause states the circumstances in which a referral to the *tribunal* can be made. That Party should notify the other Party of his intention to refer, he cannot refer the dispute to the *tribunal* within four weeks of such notification of intention, and then can only refer after any dispute resolution procedure stated in the Scope has been concluded.

Stage A   How a *Client* invites tenders for a job

Example A1   Title page

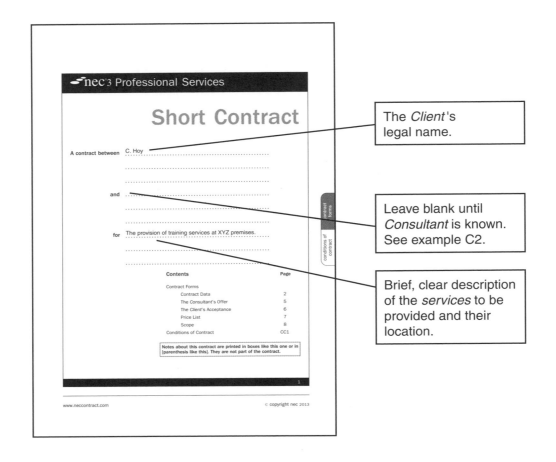

The *Client*'s legal name.

Leave blank until *Consultant* is known. See example C2.

Brief, clear description of the *services* to be provided and their location.

Example A2   Contract Data

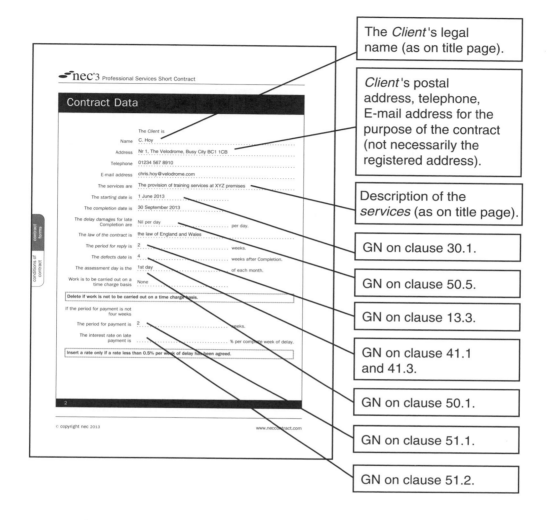

nec3 Professional Services Short Contract

Contract Data

The *Client* is

Name	C. Hoy
Address	Nr 1, The Velodrome, Busy City BC1 1CB
Telephone	01234 567 8910
E-mail address	chris.hoy@velodrome.com
The *services* are	The provision of training services at XYZ premises
The *starting date* is	1 June 2013
The *completion date* is	30 September 2013
The delay damages for late Completion are	Nil per day .... per day.
The *law of the contract* is	the law of England and Wales
The *period for reply* is	2 .... weeks.
The *defects date* is	4 .... weeks after Completion.
The *assessment day* is the	1st day .... of each month.
Work is to be carried out on a time charge basis	None

Delete if work is not to be carried out on a time charge basis.

If the period for payment is not four weeks	
The *period for payment* is	2 .... weeks.
The interest rate on late payment is	.... % per complete week of delay.

Insert a rate only if a rate less than 0.5% per week of delay has been agreed.

2

© copyright nec 2013   www.neccontract.com

Boxes pointing to the form:

- The *Client*'s legal name (as on title page).
- *Client*'s postal address, telephone, E-mail address for the purpose of the contract (not necessarily the registered address).
- Description of the *services* (as on title page).
- GN on clause 30.1.
- GN on clause 50.5.
- GN on clause 13.3.
- GN on clause 41.1 and 41.3.
- GN on clause 50.1.
- GN on clause 51.1.
- GN on clause 51.2.

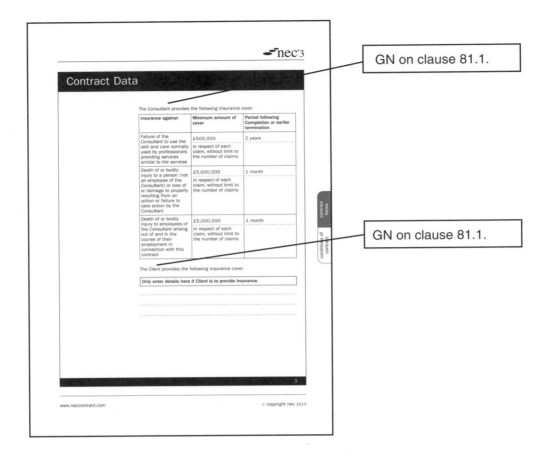

GN on clause 81.1.

GN on clause 81.1.

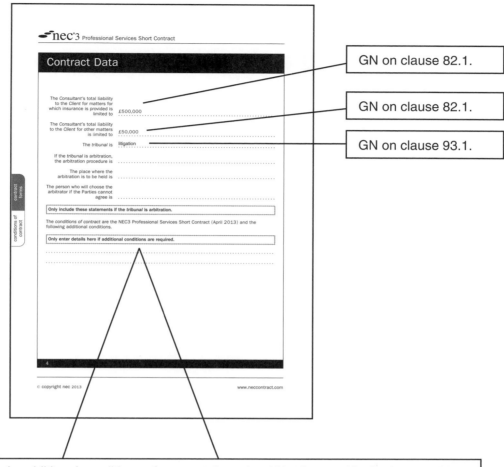

GN on clause 82.1.

GN on clause 82.1.

GN on clause 93.1.

If the *Client* needs to include additional conditions of contract they should be inserted in the box provided at the end of the Contract Data. Any additional conditions should be drafted in the same style as the PSSC clauses, using the same defined terms and other terminology. They should be carefully checked, preferably by flowcharting, to ensure that they mesh with the PSSC clauses.

Additional conditions should be used only when absolutely necessary to accommodate special needs which are not covered by the PSSC clauses. Such special needs may be those particular to the country where the work is to be done.

See notes on additional compensation events under clause 60.1.

Many special needs can be accommodated during the invitation to tender, by insertions in the Scope and by appropriate use of the Price List.

Stage B How a tenderer makes an offer

Example B1   The *Consultant*'s Offer

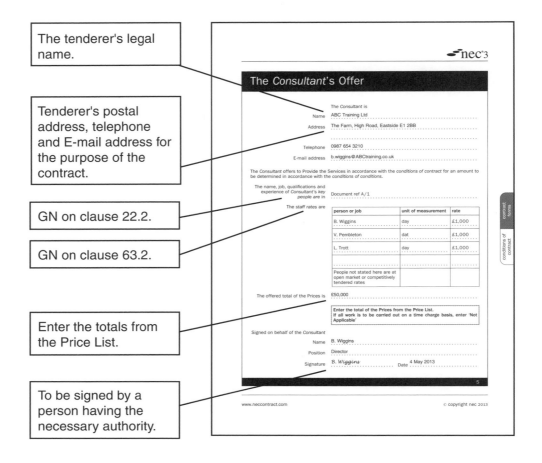

The tenderer's legal name.

Tenderer's postal address, telephone and E-mail address for the purpose of the contract.

GN on clause 22.2.

GN on clause 63.2.

Enter the totals from the Price List.

To be signed by a person having the necessary authority.

nec·3

The *Consultant*'s Offer

The *Consultant* is
Name ABC Training Ltd
Address The Farm, High Road, Eastside E1 2BB

Telephone 0987 654 3210
E-mail address b.wiggins@ABCtraining.co.uk

The *Consultant* offers to Provide the Services in accordance with the *conditions of contract* for an amount to be determined in accordance with the *conditions of conditions*.

The name, job, qualifications and experience of *Consultant's key people are in*   Document ref A/1

The *staff rates* are

person or job	unit of measurement	rate
B. Wiggins	day	£1,000
V. Pembleton	dat	£1,000
L. Trott	day	£1,000
People not stated here are at open market or competitively tendered rates		

The offered total of the Prices is   £50,000

Enter the total of the Prices from the Price List.
If all work is to be carried out on a time charge basis, enter 'Not Applicable'

Signed on behalf of the *Consultant*
Name B. Wiggins
Position Director
Signature B. *Wiggins*   Date 4 May 2013

5

www.neccontract.com   © copyright nec 2013

Left blank until completed at a later stage by the *Client*. See example C1.

━●━nec®3 Professional Services Short Contract

The *Client*'s Acceptance

The *Client* accepts the *Consultant*'s Offer to Provide the Services

Signed on behalf of the *Client* ....

Name ....

Position ....

Signature .... Date ....

contract forms

conditions of contract

6

© copyright nec 2013   www.neccontract.com

Stage C   How a contract is made

Example C1   The *Client*'s acceptance

**Stage C
How a
contract
is made**

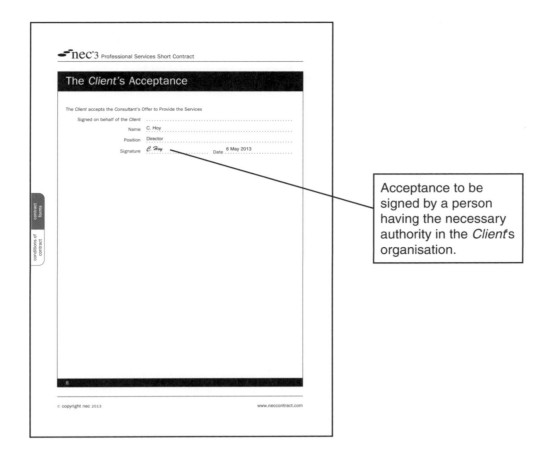

Acceptance to be signed by a person having the necessary authority in the *Client*'s organisation.

Example C2   Title page

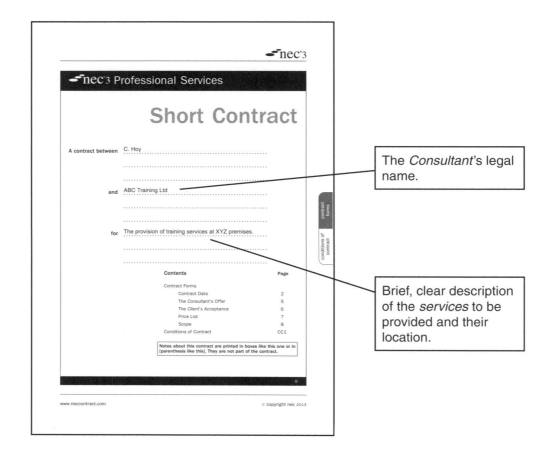

The *Consultant*'s legal name.

Brief, clear description of the *services* to be provided and their location.

EXAMPLE OF A DISPUTE RESOLUTION PROCEDURE FIXED BY LAW – WORK IN THE UK CONSTRUCTION SECTOR

If the *services* undertaken are in the UK construction sector, then the contract may have to comply with the terms of the Housing Grants, Construction and Regeneration Act (1996), as modified by the Local Democracy, Economic Development and Construction Act 2009, (the Act). While much of the works carried out under the PSSC will probably not fall within the Act, the definition of what activities and contracts the Act applies to is complex, and, if the *Client* is unsure, it is recommended that legal advice is obtained as to whether or not the Act applies.

If the Act does apply, then the parties will need to incorporate as additional conditions the clauses set out below, and agree who should be the *Adjudicator*.

In the invitation to tender there should then be a list of suggested adjudicators from which the tenderers are asked to choose one. The tenderer's covering letter would then include the tenderer's choice of adjudicator from the list suggested by the *Client* or, if none is acceptable, the tenderer's own suggestions.

The *Adjudicator* should normally be named in the final Contract Data, which would be an alteration within the standard PSSC Contract Data. Acceptance of the *Consultant*'s Offer signifies agreement to the named *Adjudicator*.

The *Adjudicator*'s impartiality and independence must be ensured. The *Adjudicator* should be a person with practical experience of the kind of *services* to be provided by the *Consultant*. The *Adjudicator* should be able to

- understand the procedures embodied in the PSSC
- understand the roles of both the *Client* and the *Consultant* in the PSSC
- act impartially and in a spirit of independence of the Parties
- understand and have access to costs at current market rates
- understand and have access to information on planning times and productivities
- appreciate risks and how allowances for them should be set and
- obtain other specialist advice when required.

Clauses 1.1 to 1.11 below will need to be written into the contract as additional conditions. These add to and change the payment and dispute resolution provisions set out in the rest of the contract.

Definitions	1.1	(1) The payment due date for an invoice submitted by the *Consultant* is the *assessment day* which follows receipt of that invoice.
		(2) The final date for payment is three weeks after the payment due date.
Assessing the amount due	1.2	The *Consultant*'s invoice is the notice of payment specifying the sum that the *Consultant* considers to be due at the payment due date (the notified sum). The *Consultant*'s invoice states the basis on which the amount is calculated and includes details of the calculation.
	1.3	If the *Client* intends to pay less than the notified sum, he notifies the *Consultant* of the amount which the *Client* considers to be due not later than seven days (the prescribed period) before the final date for payment. The *Client*'s notification states the basis on which the amount is calculated and includes details of the calculation. A Party pays the notified sum unless he has notified his intention to pay less than the notified sum.
Compensation event	1.4	If the *Consultant* exercises his right under the Act to suspend performance, it is a compensation event.

The adjudication 1.5 A Party may issue to the other Party a notice of his intention to refer a dispute to adjudication at any time. He refers the dispute to the *Adjudicator* within 7 days of the notice.

1.6 The *Adjudicator* reaches a decision within

- 28 days of the referral,
- such longer time that the Parties have agreed after the referral or
- 42 days of the referral with the consent of the Party who referred the dispute to the *Adjudicator*.

1.7 The *Adjudicator* acts impartially. The *Adjudicator*'s decision is binding until the dispute is finally determined by legal proceedings, by arbitration or by agreement.

1.8 The *Adjudicator* is not liable for anything done or omitted unless in bad faith, and any employee or agent of the *Adjudicator* is similarly not liable.

1.9 The *Adjudicator* may in his decision allocate his fees and expenses between the Parties.

1.10 The *Adjudicator* may, within five days of giving his decision to the Parties, correct the decision to remove a clerical or typographical error arising by accident or omission.

1.11 If the *Adjudicator*'s decision changes an amount notified as due, payment of the sum decided by the *Adjudicator* is due not later than seven days from the date of the decision or the final date for payment of the notified amount, whichever is the later.

Some further explanation of these additional clauses is below:

1.1 In order to comply with Section 110 of the Act, this clause defines when the payment becomes due and the final date for payment.

1.2 This clause confirms that the *Consultant*'s invoice, issued in accordance with clause 50.1, is the notice of payment required by Section 110A of the Act. It is required to show the basis upon which any payment due has been calculated.

1.3 In order to comply with Section 111 of the Act it sets out the requirement that, if the *Client* wishes to pay less than the sum set out the *Consultant*'s invoice, he must give a notice setting out the amount he intends to pay and the basis upon which it has been calculated. This notice must be given at least 7 days before the final date for payment set out in clause 1.1(2). Without such notice the *Client* is required to pay the sum in the *Consultant*'s invoice.

1.4 Under Section 112 of the Act the *Consultant* has the right to suspend performance of all or any part of the *services* if

- he is not paid the amount set out in his application by the final date for payment, unless a notice to pay a lesser sum has been given in accordance with clause 1.3, or
- if a notice to pay a lesser sum has been given in accordance with clause 1.3, and that lesser sum has not been paid by the final date for payment.

If the *Consultant* exercises this right it is a compensation event.

1.5 This clause allows for adjudication to take place at any time, as required by the Act. In order to ensure the early declaration of a dispute and expedite its resolution, time limits are stated. After notification of a dispute a maximum of 7 days occurs between notification to the other Party of and intention to refer a dispute to adjudication and referring the dispute itself to the *Adjudicator*. Though a short time period, it may encourage the Parties to resolve the dispute themselves. Compliance with the time periods stated in this clause is crucially important otherwise the dispute is barred from referral to the *Adjudicator*.

1.6 The time for the *Adjudicator*'s decision is fixed, but it can be extended if necessary by agreement or with the consent of the referring Party.

1.7 This clause establishes the principle that by the *Adjudicator* is required to act impartially. The *Adjudicator*'s decision is binding unless and until it is revised by legal proceedings, by arbitration or by agreement.

1.9 This clause gives the *Adjudicator* the power to decide how to allocate his fees and expenses between the Parties. This clause, which is required by the Act, means that the Parties have agreed to implement the provision in the NEC *Adjudicator*'s Contract allowing the Parties to agree that these fees and expenses will not be shared equally.

1.10 Once the *Adjudicator* has made his decision and notified it to the Parties his role in the dispute would normally be over. This clause gives him the right to subsequently correct a clerical or typographical error which has arisen by accident or by omission, as is required by the Act.

MULTI-PARTY PARTNERING

Introduction

A partnering contract, between two Parties only, is achieved by using a standard NEC contract. If partnering is required between two or more parties working on the same project or programme of projects, then amendments are required to the PSSC. In other NEC contracts, secondary Option X12 Partnering is provided to achieve this arrangement. The PSSC does not have a secondary Options structure so a stand alone clause has been drafted using X12 as a basis. This stand alone clause is referred to as the PSSC multi-party partnering clause in this document. This clause can be used alongside other contracts using X12. Similar amendments would be necessary if the multi-party arrangement was to be extended to a subcontractor appointed using the PSSC as a subcontract.

The parties who have the PSSC multi-party partnering clause included in their contracts are all the bodies who are intended to make up the project partnering team. The PSSC multi-party partnering clause does not create a multiparty contract.

This clause does not duplicate provisions of the appropriate existing conditions of contract in the NEC family that will be used for the individual contracts. It follows normal NEC structure in that it is made up of clauses, data and information.

The content is derived from the Guide to Project Team Partnering published by the Construction Industry Council (CIC). The requirements of the CIC document that are not already in the NEC bi-party contract are covered in this clause. The structure of the NEC family of contracts means the PSSC multiparty partnering clause will not work unless an NEC contract is used.

The purpose of this clause (and Option X12 Partnering) is to establish the NEC family as an effective contract basis for multi-party partnering. As with all NEC documents it is intended that the range of application should be wide. By linking this clause (or X12) to appropriate bi-party contracts, it is intended that the NEC can be used for partnering for any number of projects (i.e. single project or multi-project),

- internationally,
- for projects of any technical composition, and
- as far down the supply chain as required.

This clause is given legal effect by including it in the appropriate bi-party contract. It is not a free standing contract but a part of each bi-party contract that is common to all contracts in a project team.

The underlying bi-party contract will be for a contribution of any type, the work content or objective of which is sufficiently defined to permit a conventional NEC contract to be signed.

Parties must recognise that by entering into a contract with the PSSC multi-party partnering clause they will be undertaking responsibilities additional to those in the basic NEC contract.

A dispute (or difference) between Partners who do not have a contract between themselves is resolved by the Core Group. This is the Group that manages the conduct of the Partners in accordance with the Partnering Information. If the Core Group is unable to resolve the issue, then it is resolved under the procedure of the Partners' Own Contracts, either directly or indirectly with the *Client*, who will always be involved at some stage in the contractual chain. The *Client* may seek to have the issues on all contracts dealt with simultaneously.

The PSSC multi-party partnering clause does not include direct remedies between non-contracting Partners to recover losses suffered by one of them caused by a failure of the other. These remedies remain available in each Partner's Own Contract, but their existence will encourage the parties to compromise any differences that arise.

This applies at all levels of the supply chain, as a *Consultant* who is a Partner retains the responsibility for actions of a subcontractor who is a Partner.

The final sanction against any Partner who fails to act as stated in the PSSC multi-party partnering clause is for the Partner who employed them not to invite them to partner again.

Additional Contract Data for the PSSC multi-party partnering clause

The *Client* is the Party for whom the projects are being carried out. He may also be the *Client* in an NEC contract.

The *Client*'s objective is the objective for the 'programme of projects' if more than one or for 'the project' if only one. The objective should be expressed quantitatively if possible (the business case). It should also include the partnering objectives.

Partnering Information includes any requirements for

- use of common information systems, sharing of offices,
- attendance at Partners' and Core Group meetings,
- participation in partnering workshops,
- arrangements for joint design development,
- value engineering and value management,
- risk management, and
- other matters that the Core Group manages.

This information should not duplicate requirements in the bi-party contracts.

The additional Contract Data for the PSSC multi-party partnering clause, like other Contract Data in the NEC contracts, does not change. The Schedule of Partners and the Schedule of Core Group Members, like the schedules referred to in the Contract Data do change from time to time. The following are samples of the typical information required in these schedules.

Schedule of Core Group Members

Date of last revision: ....

The Core Group members are the *Client* and the following.

Name of Partner	Address and contact details	Joining date	Leaving date

Including the PSSC multi-party partnering clause in the Own Contracts

This clause is given legal effect by including it in the appropriate bi-party contract. It is not a free standing contract but a part of each bi-party contract that is common to all contracts in a project team.

The underlying bi-party contract will be for a contribution of any type, the work content or objective of which is sufficiently defined to permit a conventional NEC contract to be signed.

Parties must recognise that by entering into a contract with the PSSC multi-party partnering clause they will be undertaking responsibilities additional to those in the basic NEC contract.

A dispute (or difference) between Partners who do not have a contract between themselves is resolved by the Core Group. This is the Group that manages the conduct of the Partners in accordance with the Partnering Information. If the Core Group is unable to resolve the issue, then it is resolved under the procedure of the Partners' Own Contracts, either directly or indirectly with the *Client*, who will always be involved at some stage in the contractual chain. The *Client* may seek to have the issues on all contracts dealt with simultaneously.

The PSSC multi-party partnering clause does not include direct remedies between non-contracting Partners to recover losses suffered by one of them caused by a failure of the other. These remedies remain available in each Partner's Own Contract, but their existence will encourage the parties to compromise any differences that arise.

This applies at all levels of the supply chain, as a *Consultant* who is a Partner retains the responsibility for actions of a subcontractor who is a Partner.

The final sanction against any Partner who fails to act as stated in the PSSC multi-party partnering clause is for the Partner who employed them not to invite them to partner again.

PSSC multi-party partnering

The PSSC multi-party partnering clause is incorporated into the Own Contract of a Partner as follows.

1. The additional conditions below (referred to as Z1 but should be numbered to suit) would be inserted in the 'additional conditions' provision in the Contract Data.

2. Add the following entry to the Contract Data in each bi-party contract:

    *   The *Client* is

        Name. . . . .

        Address . . . .

        . . . .

    *   The *Client*'s *objective* is . . . .

        . . . .

        . . . .

        . . . .

        . . . .

        . . . .

        . . . .

    *   The Partnering Information is in

        . . . .

        . . . .

        . . . .

        . . . .

PSSC multi-party partnering

Z1: Partnering

Identified and defined terms Z1.1

(1) The Partners are those named in the Schedule of Partners. The *Client* is a Partner.

(2) An Own Contract is a contract between two Partners which includes this clause.

(3) The Core Group comprises the Partners listed in the Schedule of Core Group Members.

(4) Partnering Information is information which specifies how the Partners work together and is either in the documents which the Contract Data states it is in or in an instruction given in accordance with this contract.

(5) A Key Performance Indicator is an aspect of performance for which a target is stated in the Schedule of Partners.

Actions Z1.2

(1) Each Partner works with the other Partners to achieve the *Client*'s objective stated in the Contract Data and the objectives of every other Partner stated in the Schedule of Partners.

(2) Each Partner nominates a representative to act for it in dealings with other Partners.

(3) The Core Group acts and takes decisions on behalf of the Partners on those matters stated in the Partnering Information.

(4) The Partners select the members of the Core Group. The Core Group decides how they will work and decides the dates when each member joins and leaves the Core Group. The *Client*'s representative leads the Core Group unless stated otherwise in the Partnering Information.

(5) The Core Group keeps the Schedule of Core Group Members and the Schedule of Partners up to date and issues copies of them to the Partners each time either is revised.

(6) This clause does not create a legal partnership between Partners who are not one of the Parties in this contract.

Working together Z1.3

(1) The Partners work together as stated in the Partnering Information and in a spirit of mutual trust and co-operation.

(2) A Partner may ask another Partner to provide information which he needs to carry out the work in his Own Contract and the other Partner provides it.

(3) Each Partner gives an early warning to the other Partners when he becomes aware of any matter that could affect the achievement of another Partner's objectives stated in the Schedule of Partners.

(4) The Partners use common information systems as set out in the Partnering Information.

(5) A Partner implements a decision of the Core Group by issuing instructions in accordance with its Own Contracts.

(6) The Core Group may give an instruction to the Partners to change the Partnering Information. Each such change to the Partnering Information is a compensation event which may lead to reduced Prices.

(7) The Core Group prepares and maintains a timetable showing the proposed timing of the contributions of the Partners. The Core Group issues a copy of the timetable to the Partners each time it is revised. The *Consultant* changes his programme if it is necessary to do so in order to comply with the revised timetable. Each such change is a compensation event which may lead to reduced Prices.

(8) A Partner gives advice, information and opinion to the Core Group and to other Partners when asked to do so by the Core Group. This advice, information and opinion relates to work that another Partner is carrying out under its Own Contract and is given fully, openly and objectively. The Partners show contingency and risk allowances in information about costs, prices and timing for future work.

(9) A Partner notifies the Core Group before subcontracting any work.

Incentives Z1.4   (1) A Partner is paid the amount stated in the Schedule of Partners if the target stated for a Key Performance Indicator is improved upon or achieved. Payment of the amount is due when the target has been improved upon or achieved and is made as part of the amount due in the Partner's Own Contract.

(2) The *Client* may add a Key Performance Indicator and associated payment to the Schedule of Partners but may not delete or reduce a payment stated in the Schedule of Partners.

Guidance notes on PSSC multi-party partnering clauses

Identified and defined terms

Clause Z1.2 (1)
The point at which someone becomes a Partner is when his Own Contract (which includes the PSSC multi-party partnering clause) comes into existence. They should then be named in the Schedule of Partners, and their representative identified.

Clause Z1.2 (3)
Not every Partner is a member of the Core Group.

Clause Z1.2 (5)
There are two options for subcontractor partners. Either the amount payable cascades down if the schedule allocates the same bonus/cost to the main contractor and subcontractor, or the main contractor absorbs the bonus/cost and does not pass it on.

Working together

Clause Z1.3 (5)
The Core Group organises and holds meetings. It produces and distributes records of each meeting which include agreed actions. Instructions from the Core Group are issued in accordance with the Partner's Own Contract. The Core Group may invite other Partners or people to a meeting of the Core Group.

Clause Z1.3 (8)
The Partners should give advice and assistance when asked, and in addition whenever they identify something that would be helpful to another Partner.

Clause Z1.3 (9)
A subcontractor/subconsultant may be a Partner, but the general policy on this should be decided at the beginning of the Project. The Core Group should advise the *Consultant*/Consultant at the outset if a subcontractor/subconsultant is to be asked to be a Partner. A subcontractor/subconsultant who the Core group decides should be a Partner should not be appointed if he is unwilling to be a Partner.

Possible alternative incentive KPI

Incentives

Clause Z1.4 (1) (also 'Z1.1 (1) and Z1.3 (3)')

If one Partner lets the others down for a particular target by poor performance, then all lose their bonus for that target. If the *Client* tries to prevent a target being met, he is in breach of clause 10.1.

There can be more than one KPI for each partner. KPIs may apply to one Partner, to several partners or to all partners.

An example of a KPI

KPI	Number of days to complete each floor of the building framework
Target	14 days
Measurement	Number of days between removal of falsework from the entire slab and from the slab below
Amount	Main contractor – £5,000 each floor Formwork and concrete sub-contractor – £2,000 each floor Structural designer – £750 each floor

Clause Z1.4 (2)

The *Client* should consult with the other Partners before adding a KPI. The effect on subcontracted work should be noted; adding a KPI to work which is subcontracted can involve a change to the KPI for a subcontractor/subconsultant.

Incentives	KPI ability of *Consultant* to complete repair works correctly first time – only applied to *Consultant*
Target	5%
Measurement	Number of recalls arising from defective or incomplete work expressed as a percentage of the number of repairs completed
Amount	0.05% of relevant component of main contract (NEC3 Term Service Contract) Price for Services Provided to Date for repairs

PROJECT BANK ACCOUNT

The *Consultant* may be included in the Project Bank Account (PBA) arrangements in the *Client*'s contract with his employer. If so, assuming the project is an *Employer* and a *Contractor* entering into a contract for *works* using the ECC, the following clauses and Deeds should be included as an additional condition in the Contract Data. Alternatively, if the project is an *Employer* and a *Consultant* entering into a contract for *services* using the PSC, the following clauses and Deeds should be used as the basis for writing an additional condition in the Contract Data.

The PBA is established and maintained by the *Client*. Amounts due to the *Consultant* are paid into the Project Bank by the *Client* and his employer, and payment to the *Consultant* is made by the Project Bank.

The Trust Deed is intended to allow payment to the *Consultant* to continue in the event of the insolvency of the *Client*. The deed is executed by the *Client* and his employer, the *Consultant*, and other consultants or subcontractors to the *Client*. The *Consultant* will sign the Trust Deed when he has been identified in the *Client*'s contract with his employer, or sign the Joining Deed if added later.

1: Project Bank Account

Definitions	1.1	(1) Project Bank Account is the account established by the *Client* and used to make payments to the *Consultant*.
		(2) Trust Deed is an agreement in the form set out in the contract which contains provisions for administering the Project Bank Account.
		(3) Joining Deed is an agreement in the form set out in the contract under which the *Consultant* joins the Trust Deed.
Payments	1.2	The *Consultant* receives payment from the Project Bank Account of the amount due from the *Client* as soon as practicable after the Project Bank Account receives payment.
	1.3	A payment which is due from the *Consultant* to the *Client* is not made through the Project Bank Account.
Effect of payment	1.4	Payments made from the Project Bank Account are treated as payments from the *Client* to the *Consultant* in accordance with this contract.

If the *Consultant* is identified as a Named Supplier in the Contract Data for the *Client*'s contract with his employer

Trust Deed	1.5	The *Client*, his employer and the *Consultant* sign the Trust Deed before the first assessment date in the contract between the *Contractor* and his employer.

If the *Consultant* is added as a Named Supplier after the *Client*'s contract with his employer came into existence

Trust Deed	1.5	The *Client*, his employer and the *Consultant* sign the Joining Deed before the first *assessment day*.
Termination	1.6	If the *Client* issues a termination certificate, no further payment is made into the Project Bank Account.

Trust Deed

This agreement is made between the *Employer,* the *Contractor* and the Named Suppliers.

Terms in this deed have the meanings given to them in the contract between .... and .... for .... (the *works*).

Background

The *Employer* and the *Contractor* have entered into a contract for the *works.*

The Named Suppliers have entered into contracts with the *Contractor* or a Subcontractor in connection with the *works.*

The *Contractor* has established a Project Bank Account to make provision for payment to the *Contractor* and the Named Suppliers.

Agreement

The parties to this deed agree that

- sums due to the *Contractor* and Named Suppliers and set out in the Authorisation are held in trust in the Project Bank Account by the *Contractor* for distribution to the *Contractor* and Named Suppliers in accordance with the banking arrangements applicable to the Project Bank Account,
- further Named Suppliers may be added as parties to this deed with the agreement of the *Employer* and *Contractor.* The agreement of the *Employer* and *Contractor* is treated as agreement by the Named Suppliers who are parties to this deed,
- this deed is subject to the law of the contract for the *works,*
- the benefits under this deed may not be assigned.

Executed as a deed on ....

by

.... (*Employer*)

.... (*Contractor*)

....

....

....

....

(Named Suppliers)

Joining Deed

This agreement is made between the *Employer,* the *Contractor* and .... (the Additional Supplier).

Terms in this deed have the meanings given to them in the contract between .... and .... for .... (the *works*).

Background

The *Employer* and the *Contractor* have entered into a contract for the *works.*

The Named Suppliers have entered into contracts with the *Contractor* or a Subcontractor in connection with the *works.*

The *Contractor* has established a Project Bank Account to make provision for payment to the *Contractor* and the Named Suppliers.

The *Employer,* the *Contractor* and the Named Suppliers have entered into a deed as set out in Annex 1 (the Trust Deed), and have agreed that the Additional Supplier may join that deed.

Agreement

The Parties to this deed agree that

* the Additional Supplier becomes a party to the Trust Deed from the date set out below,
* this deed is subject to the law of the contract for the *works,*
* the benefits under this deed may not be assigned.

Executed as a deed on ....

by

.... (*Employer*)

.... (*Contractor*)

.... (Additional Supplier)

Flow charts for the

Professional Services Short Contract

FLOW CHARTS

PREFACE

These flow charts depict the procedures followed when using the NEC3 Professional Services Short Contract (PSSC). They are intended to help people using the PSSC to see how the various PSSC clauses produce clear and precise sequences of action for the people involved.

The flow charts are not part of any contract. Much of the text and many of the words taken from the PSSC itself are abbreviated in the flow charts. The flow charts depict almost all of the sequences of action set out in the PSSC. Many of the sequences interact, and because of this, users of the flow charts will often have to review more than one sheet in order to track the full sequence of actions in one area.

ABBREVIATIONS USED IN THE FLOW CHART BOXES

FC 16	Flow chart for clause 16
C	*Consultant*
Cl	*Client*
SC	Subconsultant
CD	Contract Data
CE	Compensation event

Legend

CHART START

HEADINGS

    Headings in caps
    provide guidance

STATEMENTS

    If a clause is
    referenced, text
    is from the NEC

LOGIC LINKS

    Links go to right
    and/or downward
    unless shown

QUESTION

    Answer question
    to determine the
    route to follow

SUBROUTINE

    Include another
    flow chart here

CONTINUATION

    Link to matching
    point(s) on other
    chart sheets

Start

HELPFUL HEADING

Statement explaining next step

Clause or
Statement using part or all of the NEC text in clause

Does this clause apply? YES

NO

FC or Description

A
sheet 2

B
sheet 2

CHART TITLE

    Chart number,
    title and sheet

**Flow chart or Sheet 1 of 2
Description**

CONTINUATION

A
sheet 2

B
sheet 2

CHART FINISH

Finish

CHART TITLE

**Flow chart or Sheet 2 of 2
Description**

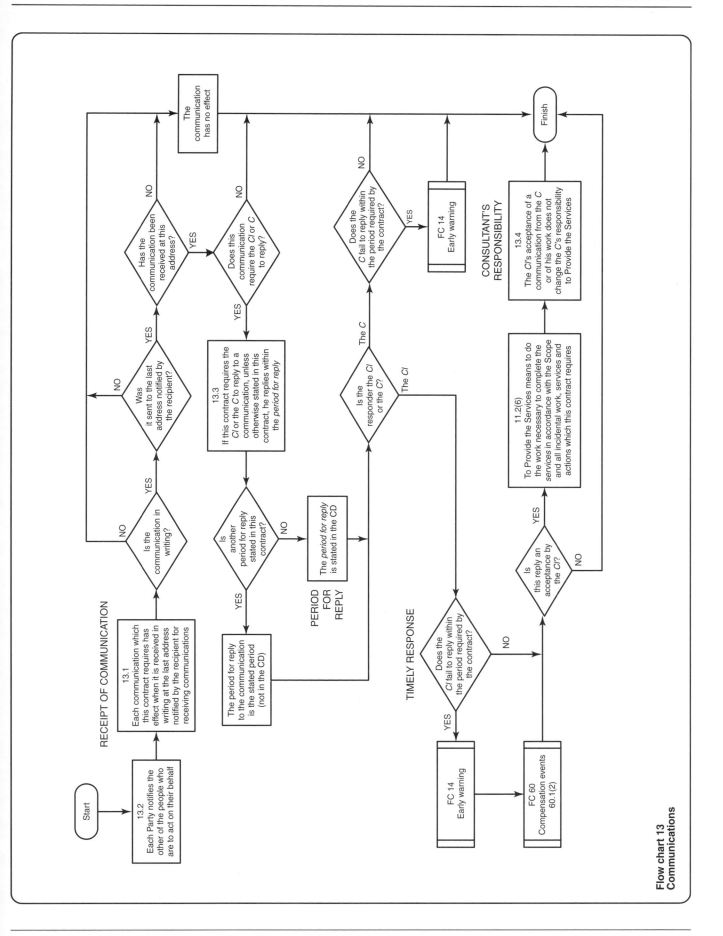

Flow chart 13
Communications

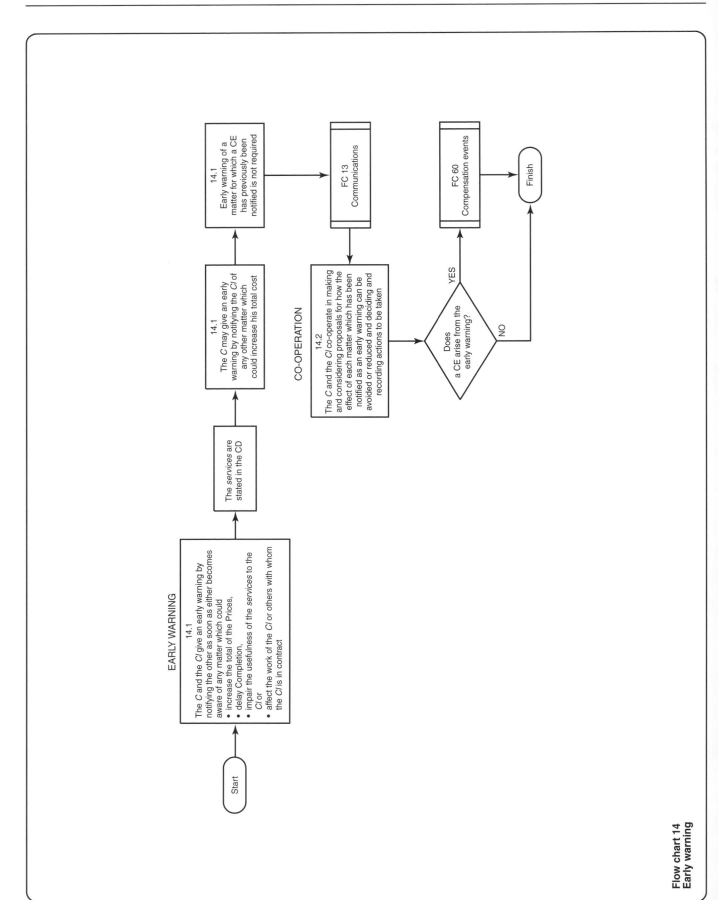

Flow chart 14
Early warning

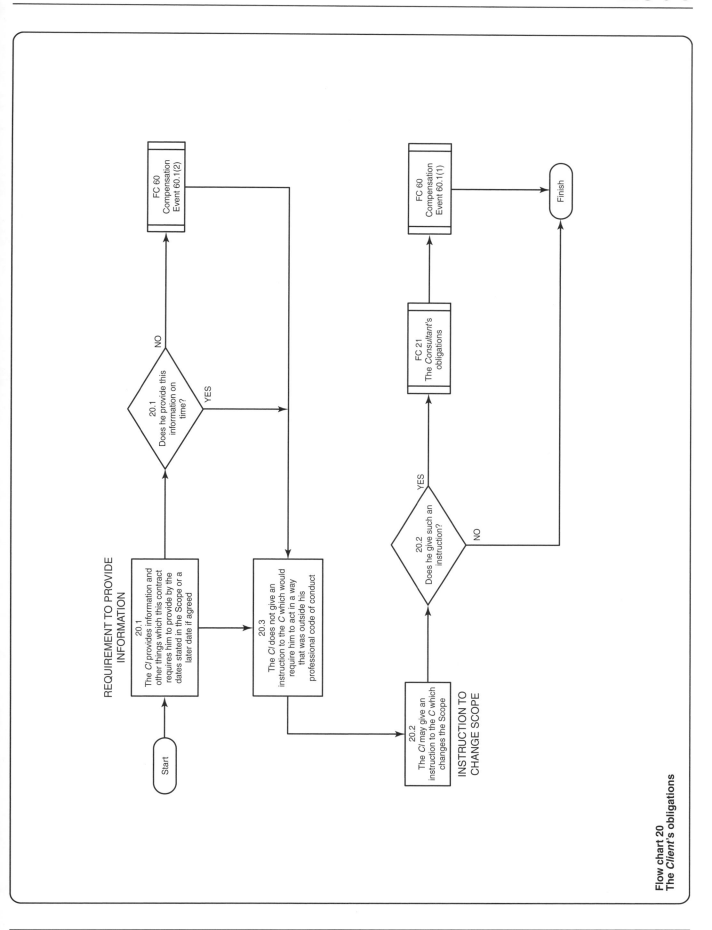

REQUIREMENT TO PROVIDE
INFORMATION

Start

20.1
The *CI* provides information and
other things which this contract
requires him to provide by the
dates stated in the Scope or a
later date if agreed

20.1
Does he provide this
information on
time?

NO

YES

FC 60
Compensation
Event 60.1(2)

20.3
The *CI* does not give an
instruction to the *C* which would
require him to act in a way
that was outside his
professional code of conduct

INSTRUCTION TO
CHANGE SCOPE

20.2
The *CI* may give an
instruction to the *C* which
changes the Scope

20.2
Does he give such an
instruction?

YES

NO

FC 21
The *Consultant's*
obligations

FC 60
Compensation
Event 60.1(1)

Finish

Flow chart 20
The *Client's* obligations

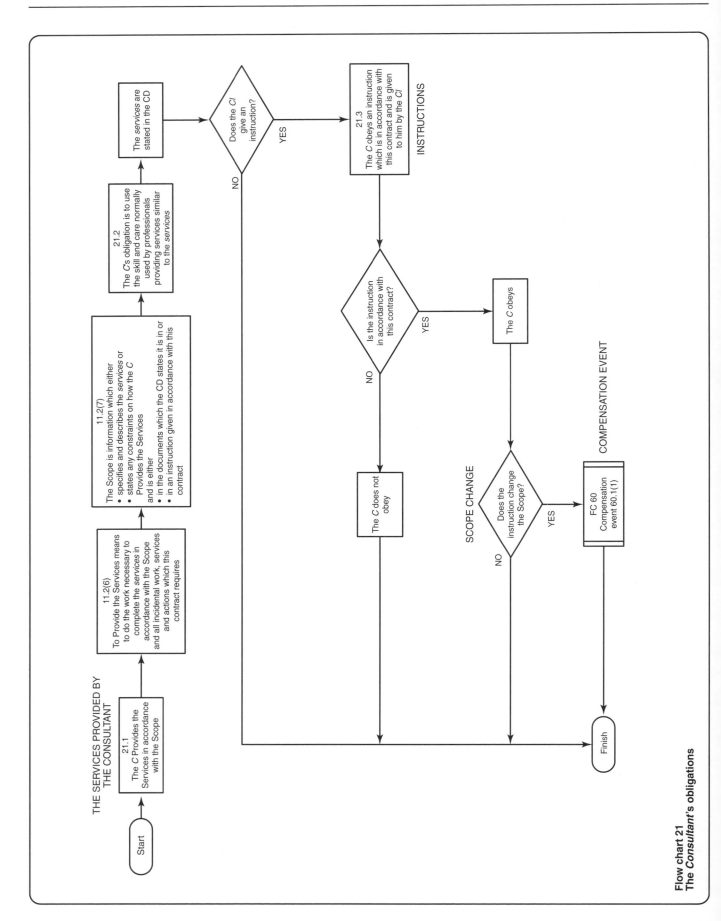

THE SERVICES PROVIDED BY
THE CONSULTANT

Start

21.1
The C Provides the
Services in accordance
with the Scope

11.2(6)
To Provide the Services means
to do the work necessary to
complete the *services* in
accordance with the Scope
and all incidental work, services
and actions which this
contract requires

11.2(7)
The Scope is information which either
• specifies and describes the *services* or
• states any constraints on how the C
  Provides the Services
and is either
• in the documents which the CD states it is in or
• in an instruction given in accordance with this
  contract

21.2
The C's obligation is to use
the skill and care normally
used by professionals
providing services similar
to the *services*

The *services* are
stated in the CD

Does the *CI*
give an
instruction?

NO

YES

21.3
The C obeys an instruction
which is in accordance with
this contract and is given
to him by the *CI*

INSTRUCTIONS

Is the instruction
in accordance with
this contract?

NO

YES

The C does not
obey

The C obeys

SCOPE CHANGE

Does the
instruction change
the Scope?

NO

YES

FC 60
Compensation
event 60.1(1)

COMPENSATION EVENT

Finish

Flow chart 21
The *Consultant*'s obligations

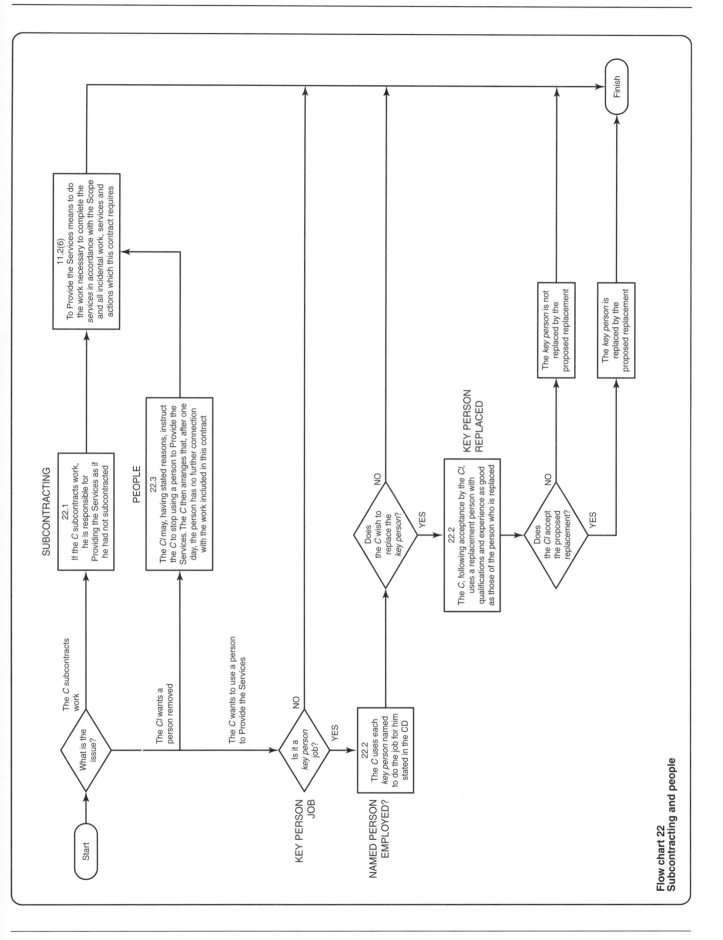

Start

What is the issue?

The C subcontracts work

The CI wants a person removed

The C wants to use a person to Provide the Services

SUBCONTRACTING

22.1
If the C subcontracts work, he is responsible for Providing the Services as if he had not subcontracted

11.2(6)
To Provide the Services means to do the work necessary to complete the services in accordance with the Scope and all incidental work, services and actions which this contract requires

PEOPLE

22.3
The CI may, having stated reasons, instruct the C to stop using a person to Provide the Services. The C then arranges that, after one day, the person has no further connection with the work included in this contract

KEY PERSON JOB

Is it a key person job?

NO

YES

NAMED PERSON EMPLOYED?

22.2
The C uses each key person named to do the job for him stated in the CD

Does the C wish to replace the key person?

NO

YES

22.2
The C, following acceptance by the CI, uses a replacement person with qualifications and experience as good as those of the person who is replaced

KEY PERSON REPLACED

Does the CI accept the proposed replacement?

NO

YES

The key person is not replaced by the proposed replacement

The key person is replaced by the proposed replacement

Finish

Flow chart 22
Subcontracting and people

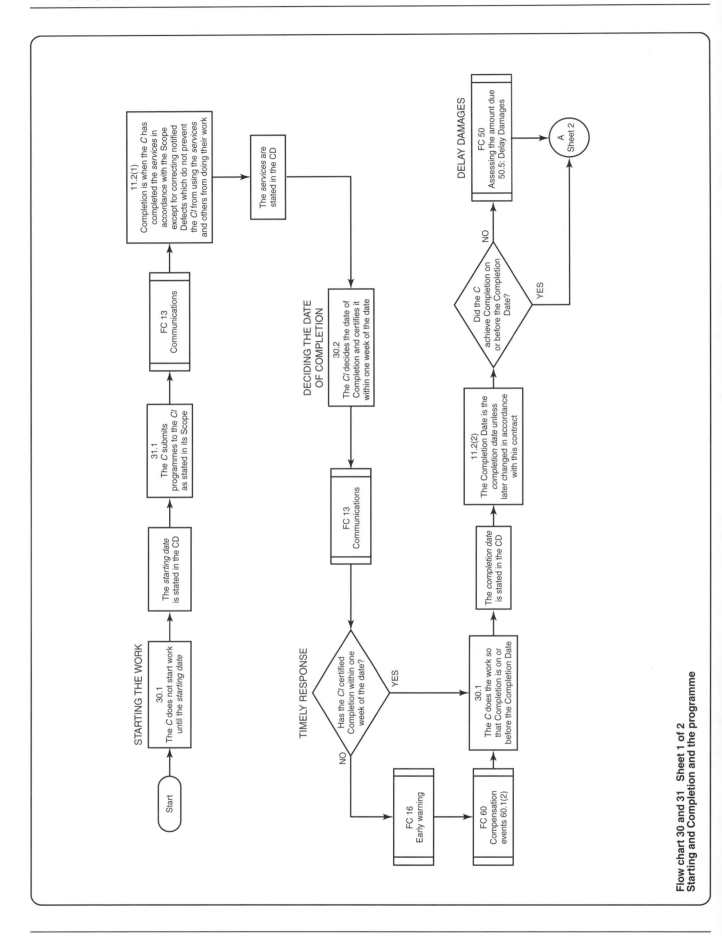

STARTING THE WORK

Start

30.1
The *C* does not start work until the *starting date*

The *starting date* is stated in the CD

31.1
The *C* submits programmes to the *CI* as stated in its Scope

FC 13
Communications

11.2(1)
Completion is when the *C* has completed the *services* in accordance with the Scope except for correcting notified Defects which do not prevent the *CI* from using the *services* and others from doing their work

The *services* are stated in the CD

DECIDING THE DATE OF COMPLETION

30.2
The *CI* decides the date of Completion and certifies it within one week of the date

FC 13
Communications

TIMELY RESPONSE

Has the *CI* certified Completion within one week of the date?

NO → FC 16
Early warning → FC 60
Compensation events 60.1(2) → 30.1
The *C* does the work so that Completion is on or before the Completion Date

YES → 30.1
The *C* does the work so that Completion is on or before the Completion Date

The *completion date* is stated in the CD

11.2(2)
The Completion Date is the *completion date* unless later changed in accordance with this contract

Did the *C* achieve Completion on or before the Completion Date?

NO → **DELAY DAMAGES**
FC 50
Assessing the amount due 50.5: Delay Damages

A
Sheet 2

YES →

Flow chart 30 and 31   Sheet 1 of 2
Starting and Completion and the programme

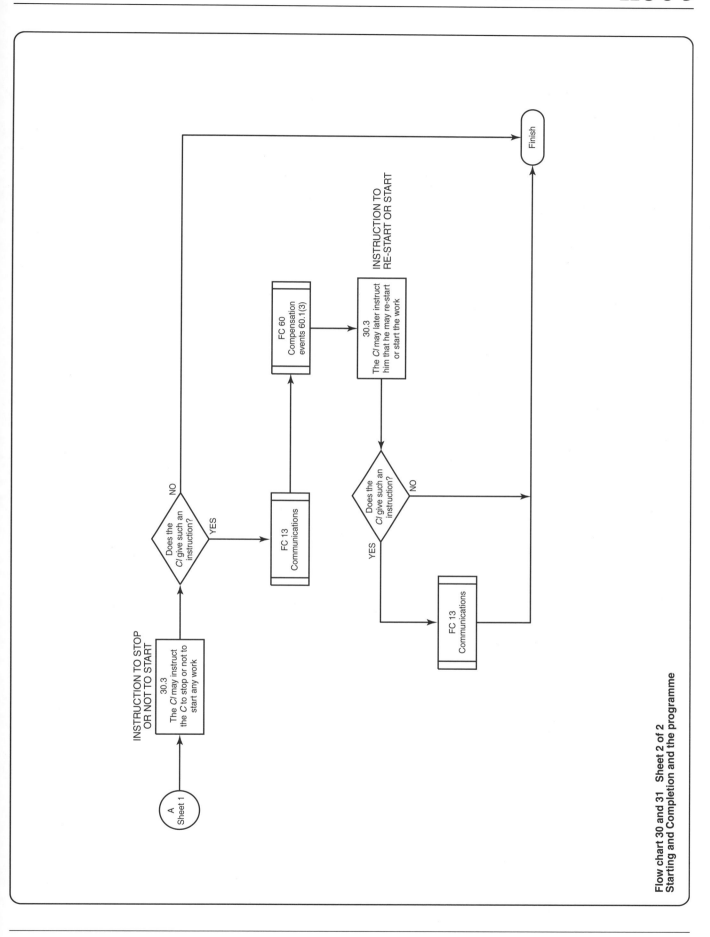

Flow chart 30 and 31 Sheet 2 of 2
Starting and Completion and the programme

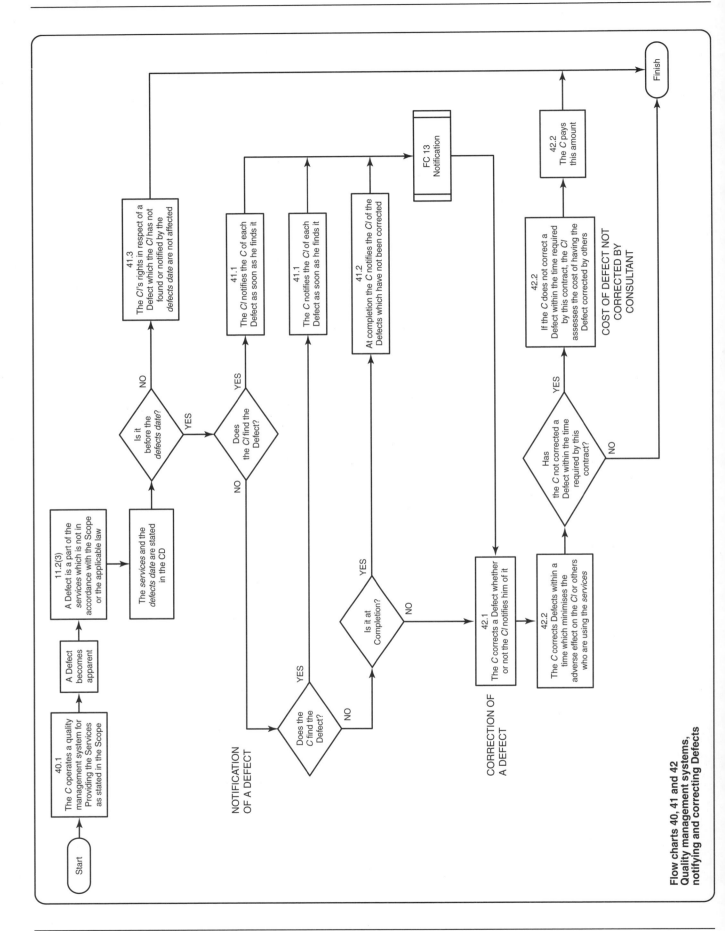

Flow charts 40, 41 and 42
Quality management systems,
notifying and correcting Defects

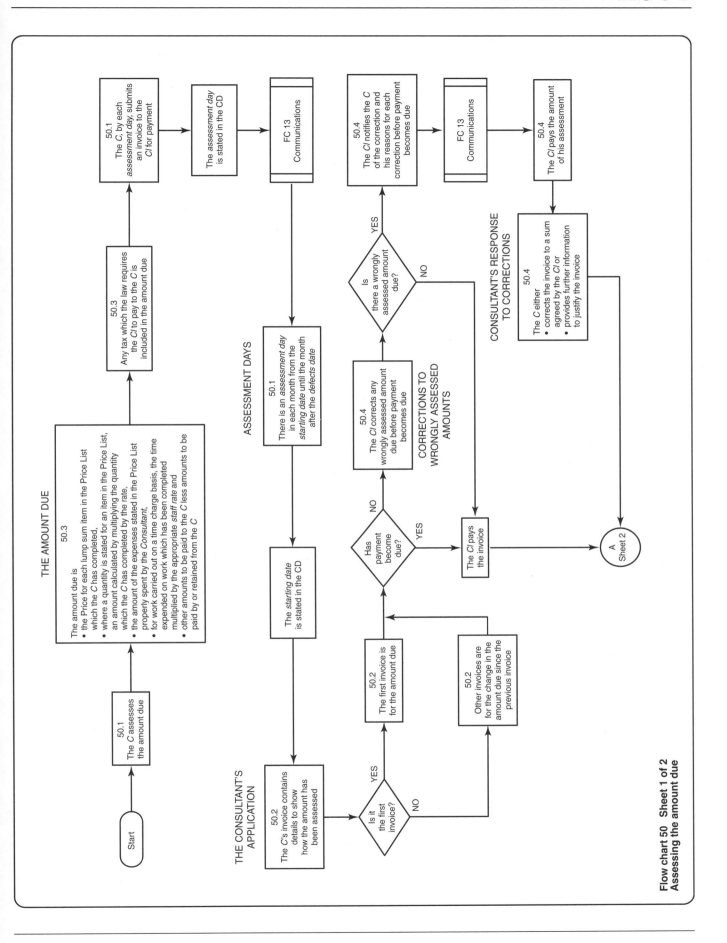

THE AMOUNT DUE

50.3
The amount due is
• the Price for each lump sum item in the Price List which the C has completed,
• where a quantity is stated for an item in the Price List, an amount calculated by multiplying the quantity which the C has completed by the rate,
• the amount of the expenses stated in the Price List properly spent by the Consultant,
• for work carried out on a time charge basis, the time expended on work which has been completed multiplied by the appropriate staff rate and
• other amounts to be paid to the C less amounts to be paid by or retained from the C

50.1
The C assesses the amount due

Start

50.3
Any tax which the law requires the Cl to pay to the C is included in the amount due

50.1
The C, by each assessment day, submits an invoice to the Cl for payment

The assessment day is stated in the CD

FC 13 Communications

ASSESSMENT DAYS

50.1
There is an assessment day in each month from the starting date until the month after the defects date

The starting date is stated in the CD

THE CONSULTANT'S APPLICATION

50.2
The C's invoice contains details to show how the amount has been assessed

Is it the first invoice?
— YES →
— NO →

50.2
The first invoice is for the amount due

50.2
Other invoices are for the change in the amount due since the previous invoice

Has payment become due?
— NO →
— YES →

50.4
The Cl corrects any wrongly assessed amount due before payment becomes due

CORRECTIONS TO WRONGLY ASSESSED AMOUNTS

Is there a wrongly assessed amount due?
— YES →
— NO →

50.4
The Cl notifies the C of the correction and his reasons for each correction before payment becomes due

FC 13 Communications

50.4
The Cl pays the amount of his assessment

CONSULTANT'S RESPONSE TO CORRECTIONS

50.4
The C either
• corrects the invoice to a sum agreed by the Cl or
• provides further information to justify the invoice

The Cl pays the invoice

A
Sheet 2

Flow chart 50   Sheet 1 of 2
Assessing the amount due

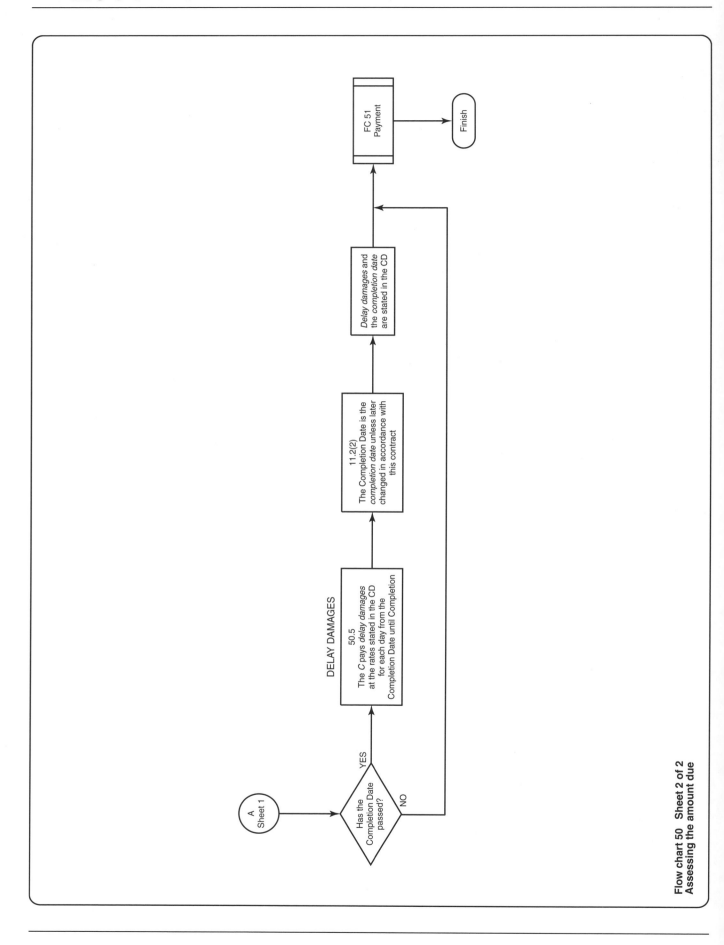

DELAY DAMAGES

50.5
The *C* pays *delay damages* at the rates stated in the CD for each day from the Completion Date until Completion

11.2(2)
The Completion Date is the *completion date* unless later changed in accordance with this contract

Delay damages and the *completion date* are stated in the CD

A
Sheet 1

Has the Completion Date passed?

YES

NO

FC 51
Payment

Finish

Flow chart 50 Sheet 2 of 2
Assessing the amount due

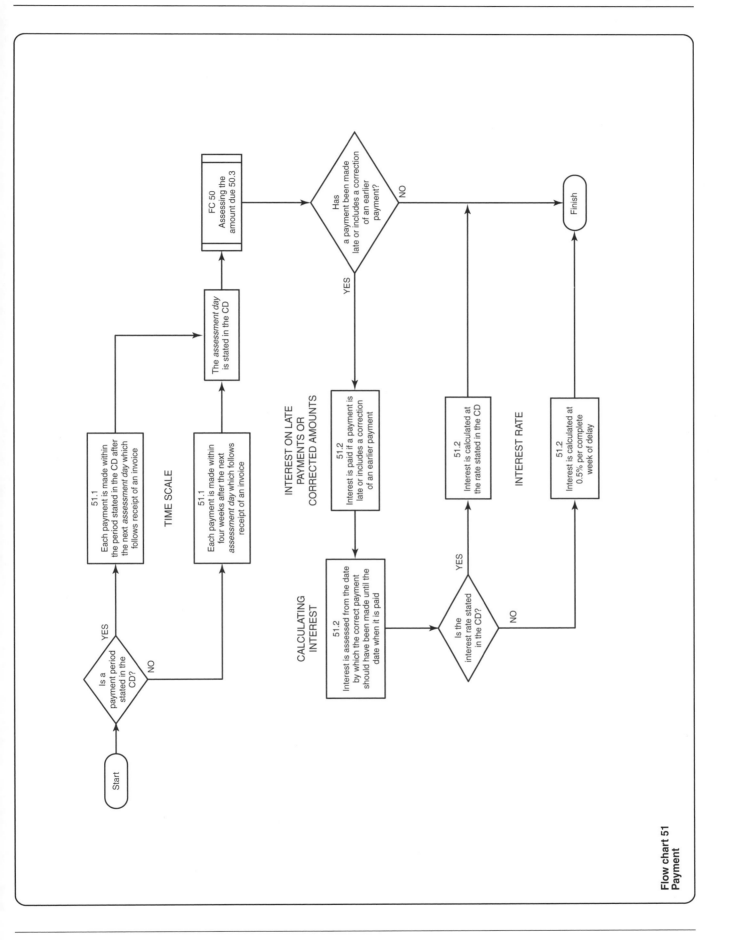

TIME SCALE

Start

Is a payment period stated in the CD?

YES → 51.1 Each payment is made within the period stated in the CD after the next assessment day which follows receipt of an invoice

NO → 51.1 Each payment is made within four weeks after the next assessment day which follows receipt of an invoice

The assessment day is stated in the CD

FC 50 Assessing the amount due 50.3

Has a payment been made late or includes a correction of an earlier payment?

YES

NO → Finish

INTEREST ON LATE PAYMENTS OR CORRECTED AMOUNTS

51.2 Interest is paid if a payment is late or includes a correction of an earlier payment

CALCULATING INTEREST

51.2 Interest is assessed from the date by which the correct payment should have been made until the date when it is paid

Is the interest rate stated in the CD?

YES → 51.2 Interest is calculated at the rate stated in the CD

NO

INTEREST RATE

51.2 Interest is calculated at 0.5% per complete week of delay

**Flow chart 51
Payment**

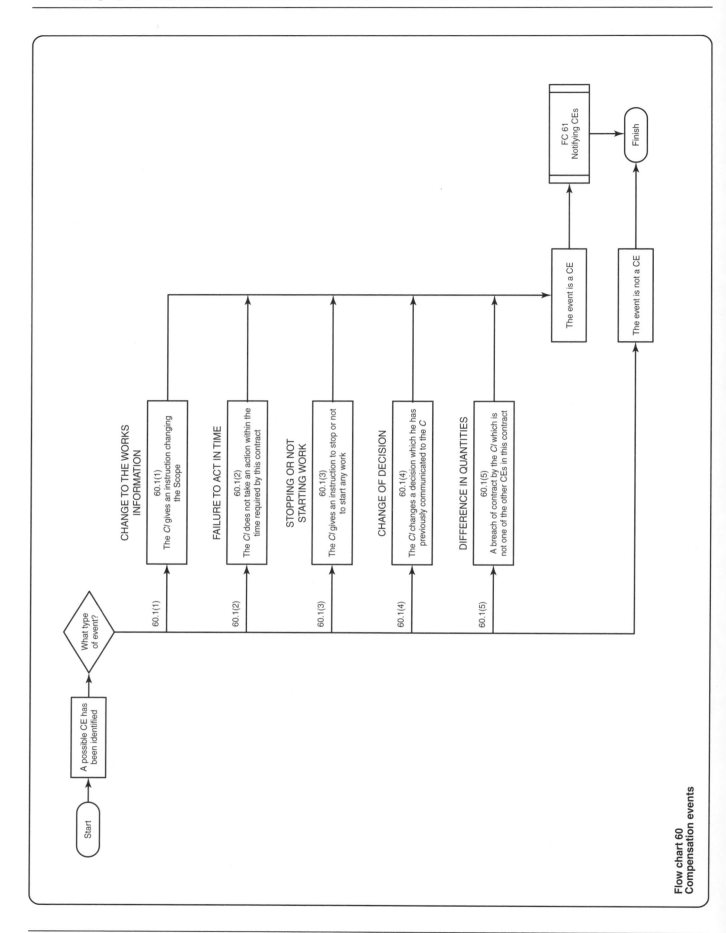

Flow chart 60
Compensation events

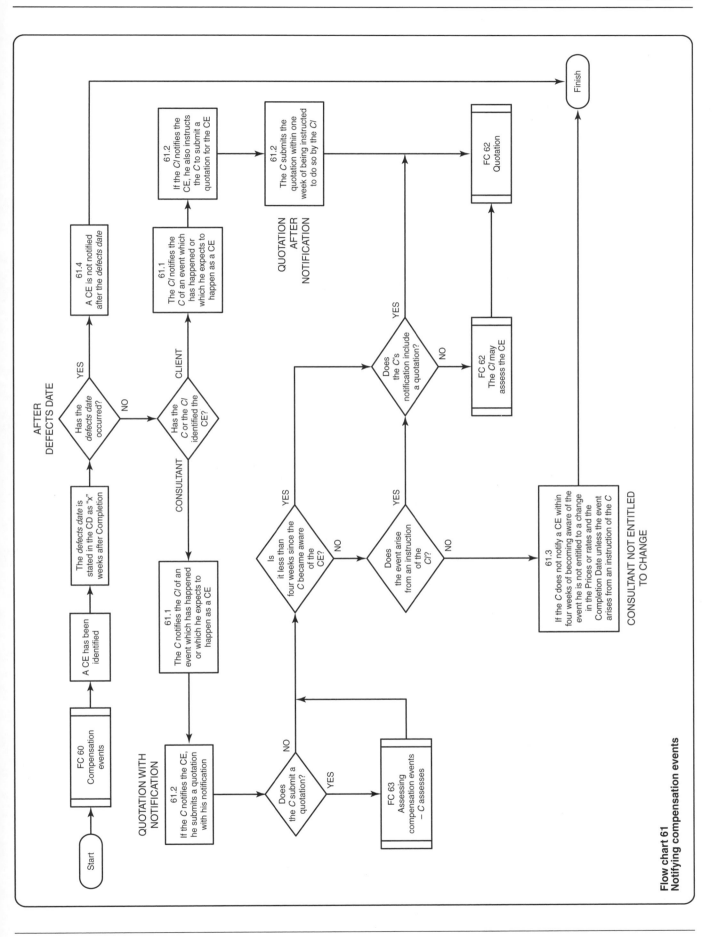

Start

FC 60
Compensation events

A CE has been identified

The *defects date* is stated in the CD as "x" weeks after Completion

AFTER DEFECTS DATE

Has the *defects date* occurred? — YES → 61.4 A CE is not notified after the *defects date*

NO

Has the *C* or the *CI* identified the CE?

CONSULTANT

CLIENT

QUOTATION WITH NOTIFICATION

61.1 The *C* notifies the *CI* of an event which has happened or which he expects to happen as a CE

61.1 The *CI* notifies the *C* of an event which has happened or which he expects to happen as a CE

61.2 If the *C* notifies the CE, he submits a quotation with his notification

61.2 If the *CI* notifies the CE, he also instructs the *C* to submit a quotation for the CE

QUOTATION AFTER NOTIFICATION

61.2 The *C* submits the quotation within one week of being instructed to do so by the *CI*

Does the *C* submit a quotation?

NO — Is it less than four weeks since the *C* became aware of the CE?

YES → FC 63 Assessing compensation events – *C* assesses

YES

NO

Does the event arise from an instruction of the *CI*?

YES

NO

61.3 If the *C* does not notify a CE within four weeks of becoming aware of the event he is not entitled to a change in the Prices or rates and the Completion Date unless the event arises from an instruction of the *C*

CONSULTANT NOT ENTITLED TO CHANGE

Does the *C's* notification include a quotation?

YES → FC 62 Quotation

NO → FC 62 The *CI* may assess the CE

Finish

**Flow chart 61
Notifying compensation events**

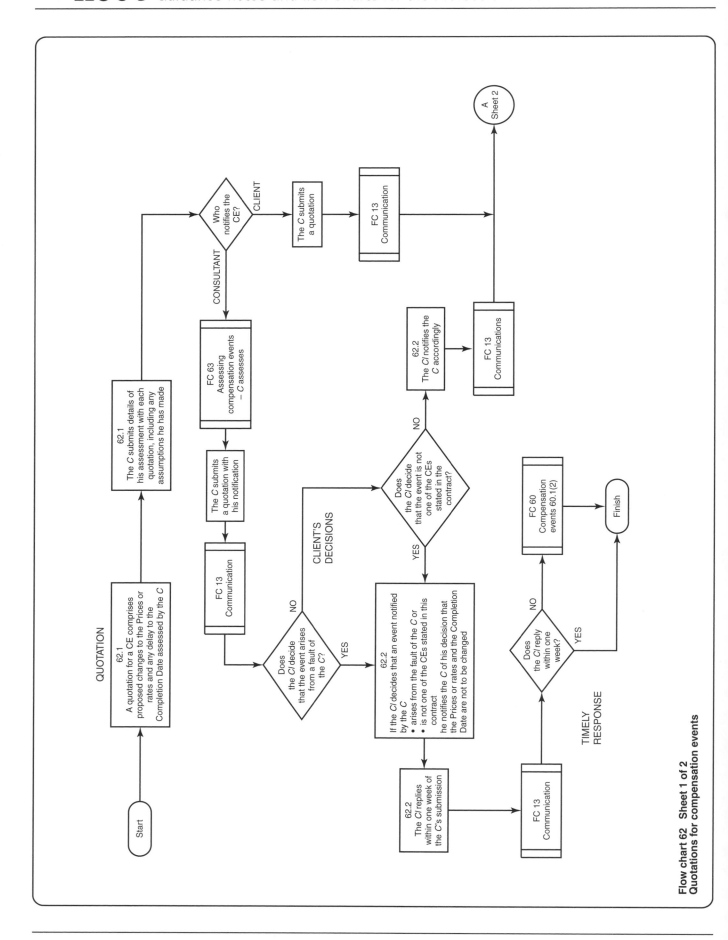

QUOTATION

62.1
A quotation for a CE comprises proposed changes to the Prices or rates and any delay to the Completion Date assessed by the C

62.1
The C submits details of his assessment with each quotation, including any assumptions he has made

Who notifies the CE?

CONSULTANT → **FC 63** Assessing compensation events – C assesses → **The C submits a quotation with his notification** → **FC 13** Communication

CLIENT → **The C submits a quotation** → **FC 13** Communication → **A Sheet 2**

CLIENT'S DECISIONS

Does the CI decide that the event arises from a fault of the C?

NO → **Does the CI decide that the event is not one of the CEs stated in the contract?**

YES → **62.2** If the CI decides that an event notified by the C
• arises from the fault of the C or
• is not one of the CEs stated in this contract
he notifies the C of his decision that the Prices or rates and the Completion Date are not to be changed

Does the CI decide that the event is not one of the CEs stated in the contract?

NO → **62.2** The CI notifies the C accordingly → **FC 13** Communications

YES → **62.2** The CI replies within one week of the C's submission → **FC 13** Communication

FC 60 Compensation events 60.1(2) → **Finish**

TIMELY RESPONSE

Does the CI reply within one week?

NO → **FC 60** Compensation events 60.1(2)

YES → **Finish**

Start

Flow chart 62 Sheet 1 of 2
Quotations for compensation events

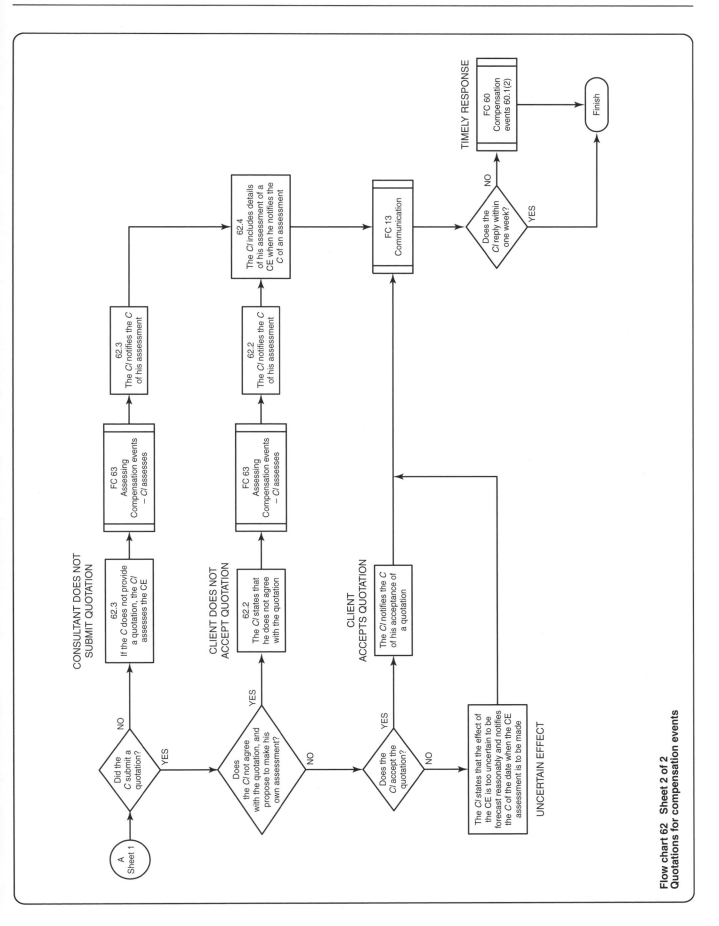

Flow chart 62   Sheet 2 of 2
Quotations for compensation events

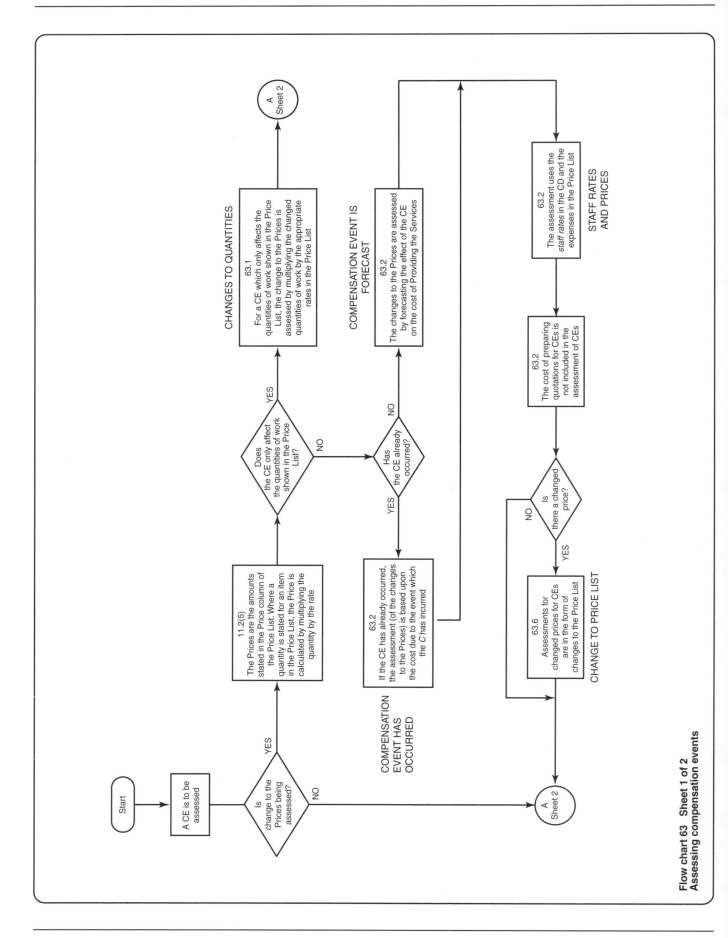

CHANGES TO QUANTITIES

63.1
For a CE which only affects the quantities of work shown in the Price List, the change to the Prices is assessed by multiplying the changed quantities of work by the appropriate rates in the Price List

COMPENSATION EVENT IS FORECAST

63.2
The changes to the Prices are assessed by forecasting the effect of the CE on the cost of Providing the Services

63.2
The assessment uses the *staff rates* in the CD and the expenses in the Price List

STAFF RATES AND PRICES

63.2
The cost of preparing quotations for CEs is not included in the assessment of CEs

11.2(5)
The Prices are the amounts stated in the Price column of the Price List. Where a quantity is stated for an item in the Price List, the Price is calculated by multiplying the quantity by the rate

Does the CE only affect the quantities of work shown in the Price List? — YES

NO

Has the CE already occurred? — YES / NO

Is there a changed price? — YES / NO

COMPENSATION EVENT HAS OCCURRED

63.2
If the CE has already occurred, the assessment (of the changes to the Prices) is based upon the cost due to the event which the *C* has incurred

63.6
Assessments for changed prices for CEs are in the form of changes to the Price List

CHANGE TO PRICE LIST

Start → A CE is to be assessed → Is change to the Prices being assessed? — YES / NO

A Sheet 2

Flow chart 63   Sheet 1 of 2
Assessing compensation events

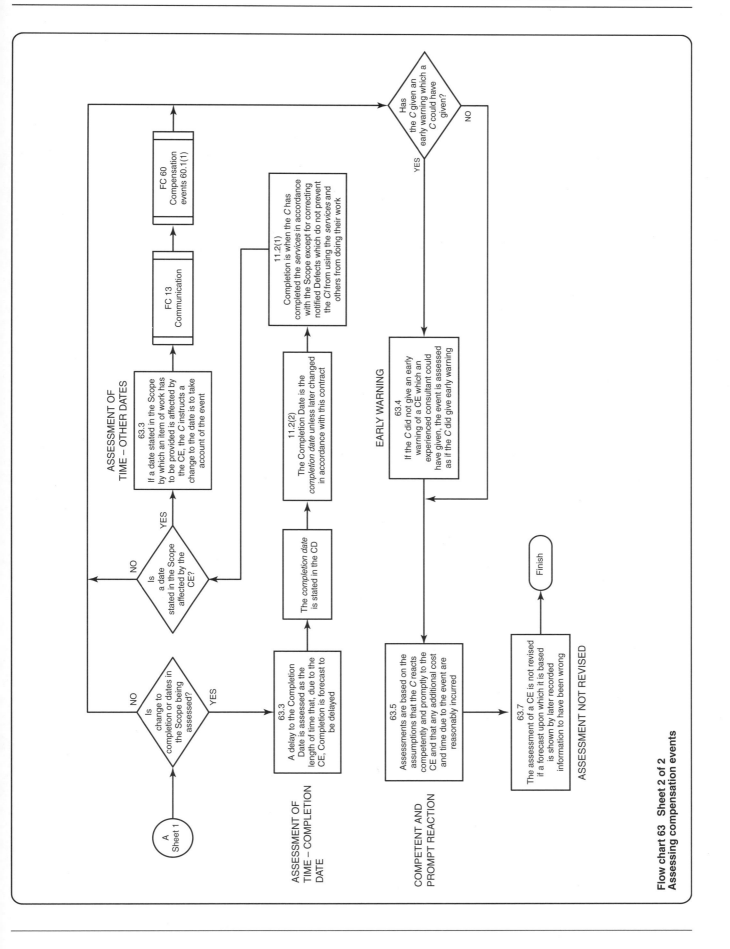

ASSESSMENT OF TIME – OTHER DATES

63.3
If a date stated in the Scope by which an item of work has to be provided is affected by the CE, the C instructs a change to the date is to take account of the event

FC 13
Communication

FC 60
Compensation events 60.1(1)

Is a date stated in the Scope affected by the CE?

NO / YES

11.2(1)
Completion is when the C has completed the *services* in accordance with the Scope except for correcting notified Defects which do not prevent the Cl from using the *services* and others from doing their work

Has the C given an early warning which a C could have given?

YES / NO

EARLY WARNING

63.4
If the C did not give an early warning of a CE which an experienced consultant could have given, the event is assessed as if the C did give early warning

ASSESSMENT OF TIME – COMPLETION DATE

Is change to completion or dates in the Scope being assessed?

NO / YES

63.3
A delay to the Completion Date is assessed as the length of time that, due to the CE, Completion is forecast to be delayed

The *completion date* is stated in the CD

11.2(2)
The Completion Date is the *completion date* unless later changed in accordance with this contract

A
Sheet 1

COMPETENT AND PROMPT REACTION

63.5
Assessments are based on the assumptions that the C reacts competently and promptly to the CE and that any additional cost and time due to the event are reasonably incurred

63.7
The assessment of a CE is not revised if a forecast upon which it is based is shown by later recorded information to have been wrong

ASSESSMENT NOT REVISED

Finish

Flow chart 63 Sheet 2 of 2
Assessing compensation events

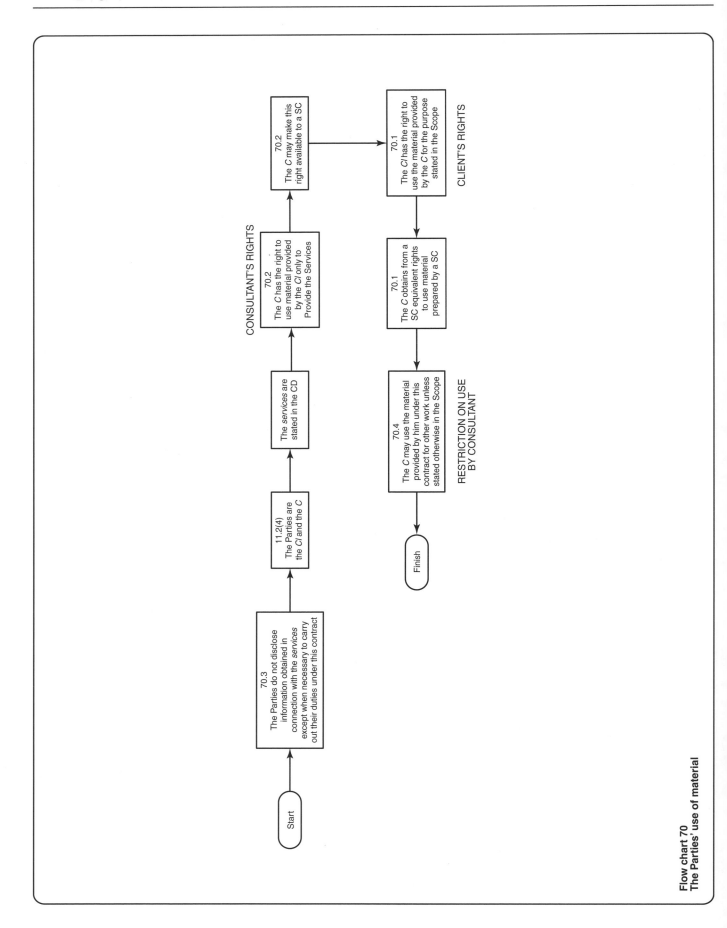
CONSULTANT'S RIGHTS

70.2
The C may make this right available to a SC

70.2
The C has the right to use material provided by the CI only to Provide the Services

The *services* are stated in the CD

11.2(4)
The Parties are the CI and the C

70.3
The Parties do not disclose information obtained in connection with the *services* except when necessary to carry out their duties under this contract

Start

CLIENT'S RIGHTS

70.1
The CI has the right to use the material provided by the C for the purpose stated in the Scope

70.1
The C obtains from a SC equivalent rights to use material prepared by a SC

RESTRICTION ON USE BY CONSULTANT

70.4
The C may use the material provided by him under this contract for other work unless stated otherwise in the Scope

Finish

Flow chart 70
The Parties' use of material

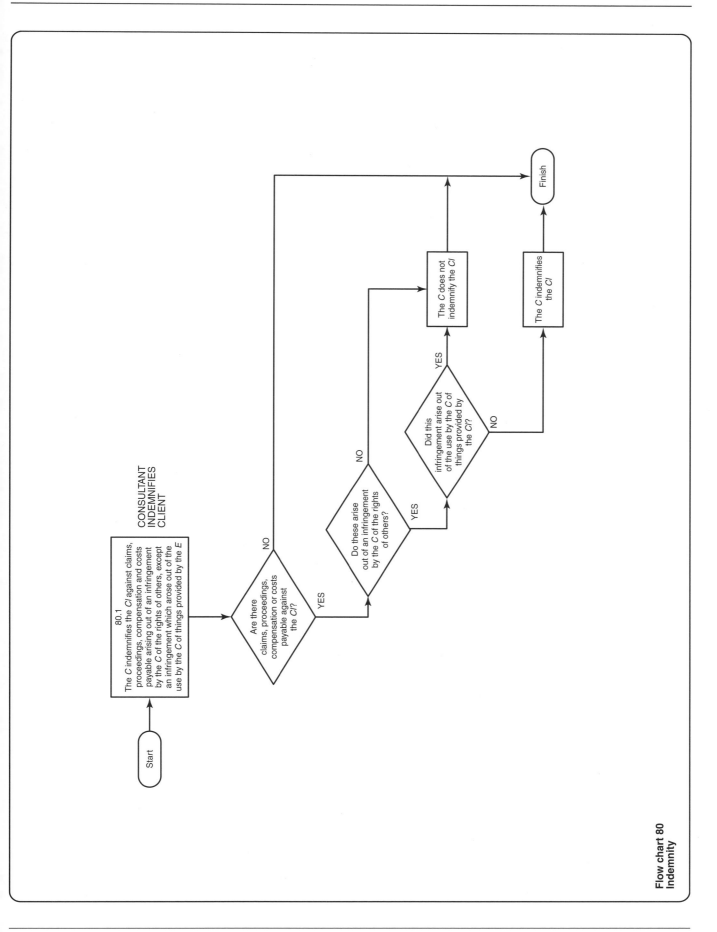

CONSULTANT INDEMNIFIES CLIENT

Start

80.1
The *C* indemnifies the *Cl* against claims, proceedings, compensation and costs payable arising out of an infringement by the *C* of the rights of others, except an infringement which arose out of the use by the *C* of things provided by the *E*

Are there claims, proceedings, compensation or costs payable against the *Cl*?

YES

NO

Do these arise out of an infringement by the *C* of the rights of others?

YES

NO

Did this infringement arise out of the use by the *C* of things provided by the *Cl*?

YES

NO

The *C* does not indemnify the *Cl*

The *C* indemnifies the *Cl*

Finish

Flow chart 80
Indemnity

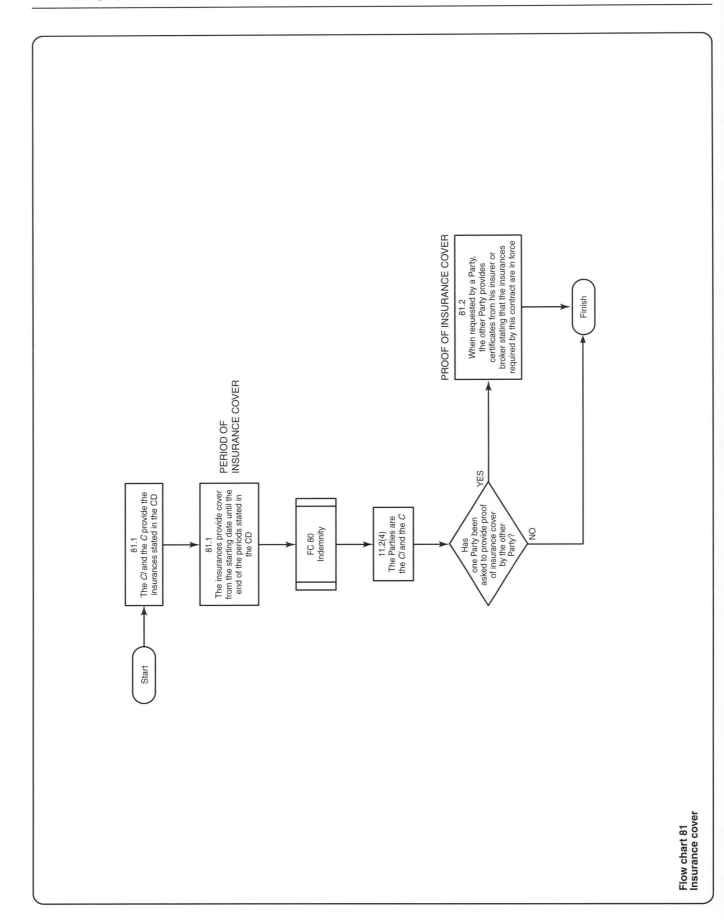

Start

81.1
The *Cl* and the *C* provide the insurances stated in the CD

PERIOD OF INSURANCE COVER

81.1
The insurances provide cover from the starting date until the end of the periods stated in the CD

FC 80
Indemnity

11.2(4)
The Parties are the *Cl* and the *C*

Has one Party been asked to provide proof of insurance cover by the other Party?

YES

NO

PROOF OF INSURANCE COVER

81.2
When requested by a Party, the other Party provides certificates from his insurer or broker stating that the insurances required by this contract are in force

Finish

Flow chart 81
Insurance cover

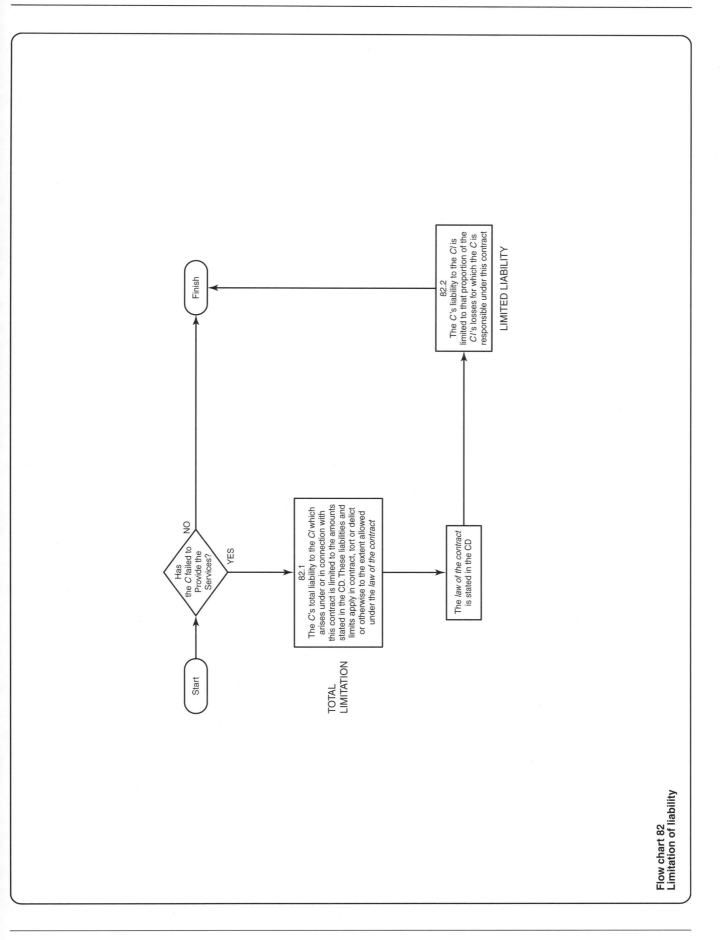

Start

Has the *C* failed to Provide the Services?

NO → Finish

YES

82.1
The *C*'s total liability to the *Cl* which arises under or in connection with this contract is limited to the amounts stated in the CD. These liabilities and limits apply in contract, tort or delict or otherwise to the extent allowed under the *law of the contract*

TOTAL LIMITATION

The *law of the contract* is stated in the CD

82.2
The *C*'s liability to the *Cl* is limited to that proportion of the *Cl*'s losses for which the *C* is responsible under this contract

LIMITED LIABILITY

→ Finish

**Flow chart 82
Limitation of liability**

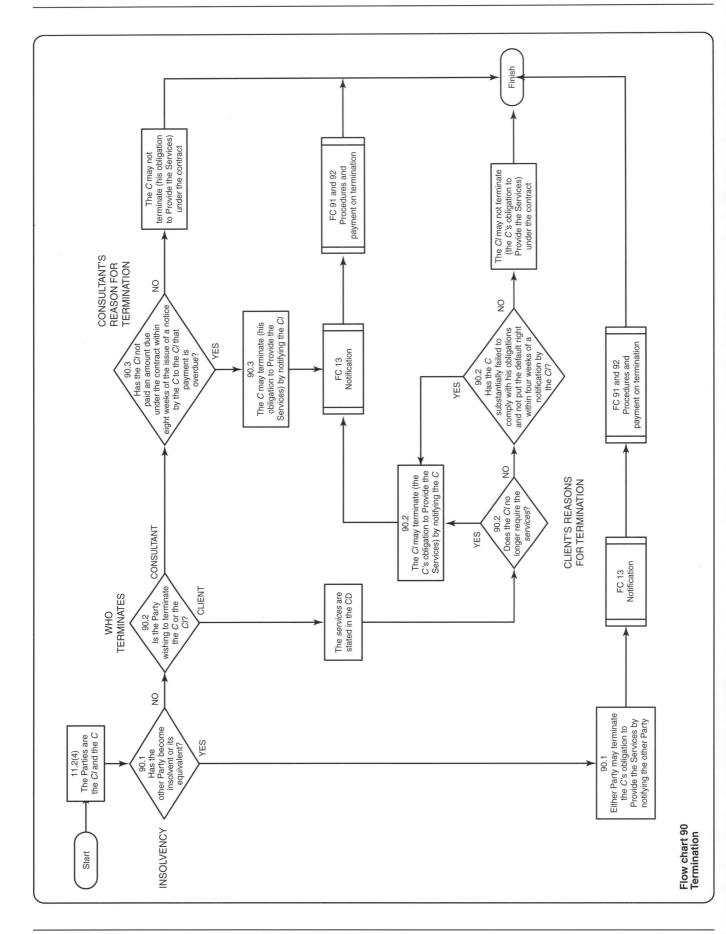

**Flow chart 90
Termination**

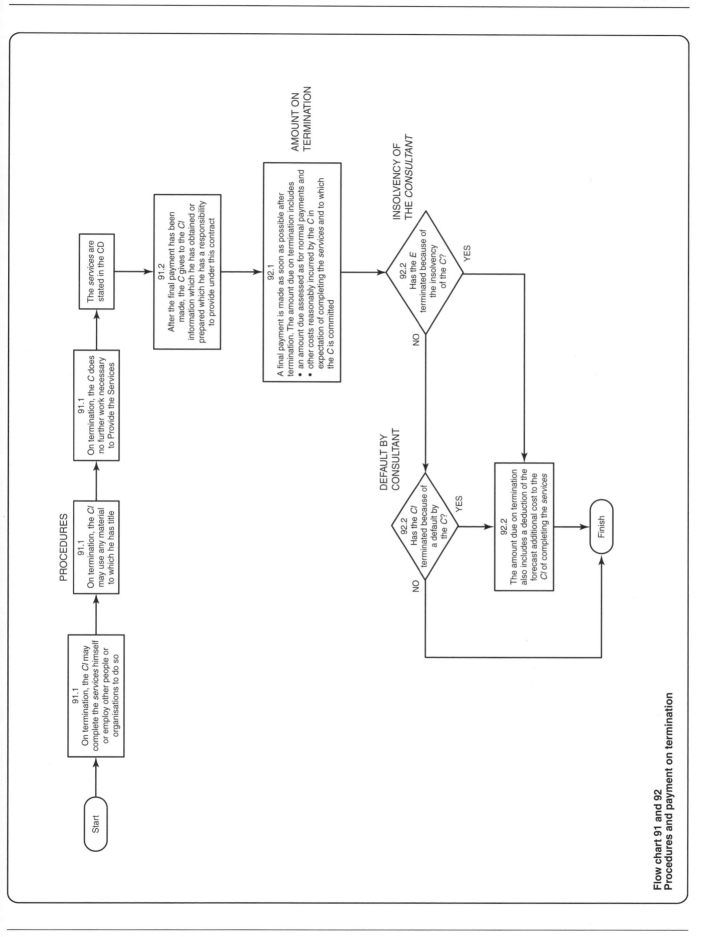

Flow chart 91 and 92
Procedures and payment on termination

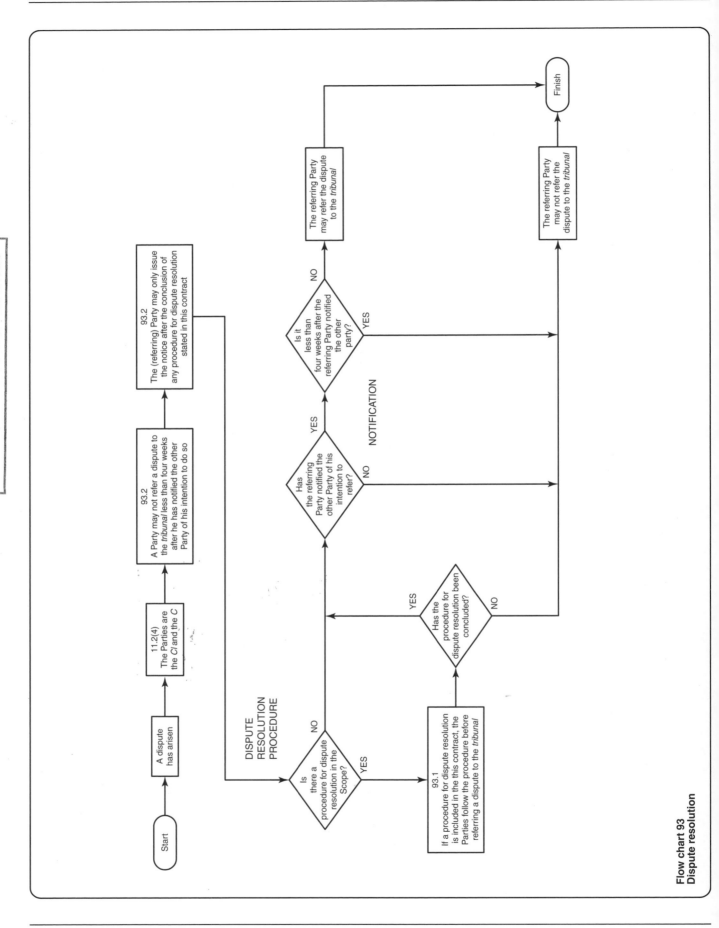

Start

A dispute
has arisen

11.2(4)
The Parties are
the *CI* and the *C*

93.2
A Party may not refer a dispute to
the *tribunal* less than four weeks
after he has notified the other
Party of his intention to do so

93.2
The (referring) Party may only issue
the notice after the conclusion of
any procedure for dispute resolution
stated in this contract

DISPUTE
RESOLUTION
PROCEDURE

Is
there a
procedure for dispute
resolution in the
Scope?

NO / YES

93.1
If a procedure for dispute resolution
is included in the this contract, the
Parties follow the procedure before
referring a dispute to the *tribunal*

Has the
procedure for
dispute resolution been
concluded?

YES / NO

Has
the referring
Party notified the
other Party of his
intention to
refer?

YES / NO

NOTIFICATION

Is it
less than
four weeks after the
referring Party notified
the other
party?

NO / YES

The referring Party
may refer the dispute
to the *tribunal*

The referring Party
may not refer the
dispute to the *tribunal*

Finish

Flow chart 93
Dispute resolution